The Thoughts
of Chairman Moore

The Thoughts of Chairman Moore

They've Kicked It Away Again

BRIAN MOORE

SIMON &
SCHUSTER

London · New York · Sydney · Toronto

A CBS COMPANY

First published in Great Britain by Simon & Schuster UK Ltd, 2010
A CBS COMPANY

Copyright © 2010 by Brian Moore

1 3 5 7 9 10 8 6 4 2

Simon & Schuster UK Ltd
1st Floor
222 Gray's Inn Road
London
WC1X 8HB

www.simonandschuster.co.uk

Simon & Schuster Australia
Sydney

A CIP catalogue for this book
is available from the British Library.

ISBN: 978-0-85720-129-4 (hardback)
978-0-85720-130-0 (trade paperback)

Typeset by M Rules
Printed in the UK by CPI Mackays, Chatham ME5 8TD

For my wife Belinda for
giving me the time and space to think
and numerous sub-editors for
bearing my frequent tirades

Introduction

Greetings, comrades.

Another famous chairman once said:

'In studying a problem, we must shun subjectivity, one-sided-ness and superficiality.'[1]

This, very loosely, describes the approach that I try to apply when writing my articles for the *Daily Telegraph*: avoid the spin and the hype and investigate the facts. From that point forward, it is possible to put into context what is being claimed or said by the protagonists in a particular matter. This often results in inconsistencies being highlighted and thus exposes those who would have us see things as they want them to be seen and not how they really are.

By at least challenging what is often vernacular wisdom, I try to help readers make up their own minds about an event by cutting through the sometimes purposely created pretence. Of course I get things wrong – and subjectivity and superficiality cannot be banished entirely – but I try to call things as they are, or at least as they are to me.

It is not possible to set out with the intention of being controversial. When your words palpably do not fit any reasonable interpretation of the facts you undermine justifiably controversial points, and readers lose faith in your ability to be objective; and once credibility is gone there is nothing left.

It is right to praise achievement and I try to balance my articles by referring to things that deserve mention. Sometimes for my

[1] ('On Contradiction' (August 1937), *Selected Works*, vol. I, pp. 323–4)

own sanity and that of my readers I just try to entertain – no one can be deeply analytical all the time without becoming a miserable bastard.

The Spanish-born philosopher George Santayana is quoted as stating: 'Those who cannot remember the past are condemned to repeat it.' Obviously I now have the benefit of hindsight when rereading these pieces and it is interesting to look back and see how many times I got it right or wrong.

What is clear to me is that, even within this limited number of articles, you can see how often people – and, more importantly, organisations – do not learn and do not remember. Ordinary sports lovers are left exasperated, shaking their heads at the latest fiasco created by those tasked with running the sport they love. It is alarming to reflect that in some sports there appears to be little or no prospect of these errors *not* being repeated.

Causing people to pause and consider a particular proposition is not always possible, but it is a decent objective. That you may not agree with my conclusions is not the point, though it is satisfying when it happens. Undoubtedly some of you will state that what I write is utter nonsense; all I strive for is to make you think about things before you reach this conclusion.

As with most anthologies, this one can be read a bit at a time; in fact, it is probably best approached in that way. And if you don't like it, remember, it also makes a good doorstop.

Brian Moore
June 2010

Author's Note

Although most of the articles are chronological, the two sections headed 'The Rain Tax' and 'Bloodgate' have been consolidated to help readers see how affairs played out, thus avoiding the need to go back and forth.

1

Have you been a good boy?

December 2007

''Tis the season to be jolly' or 'Bah humbug to you': whatever your take on festivities this week, take a look at what gifts Santa Moore has lined up for good rugby people in 2007.

For Kiwis: a slightly serious yet practical present – *A Dummies Guide to the Heimlich Manoeuvre*. This easy-to-read, step-by-step pamphlet could just save your life; okay, you might need it only once in four years, but better safe than sorry. Watch out for the new and even more comprehensive edition which will hit the shelves in 2011.

For all Aussic front rows: the Charles Atlas mail order course, 'Are you tired of getting sand kicked in your face?' This course of dynamic tension exercises will turn you from 97-pound weaklings into the world's most powerful front row. No longer do you have to accept being the butt of everyone's jokes. Following the Atlas course every day for a decade will provide you with muscles you told yourself, and everyone else, you didn't need. Guaranteed 'Sheridan-proof'.

For Brian Ashton: a Ronco 'Andrew Detector'. Effective over 50 metres, this small device will alert you to the presence of England elite rugby director Rob Andrew, enabling you to move to a different seat; never again get trapped on TV with your boss. This scientific approach to 'Andrew detection' will stop you having to rely on the old wives' tale of expecting to see him only when your team's winning.

For Lawrence Dallaglio and Mike Catt: the super new 'Retractor Kit'. This amazing product allows you instantly to retract anything you have proof-read and authorised for publication. Using a little-known piece of Government sophistry known as 'being taken out of context', the 'Retractor' will ensure you are able to make any number of contradictory statements yet still retain the public's complete confidence.

For all Wasps OAPs: if, like poor Alan Black, you are often driven almost to the point of violence by the poor value afforded you by your club's match-day programme, I can enrol you on a two-day anger management course with Harrow Social Services; much better than a lifetime ban and discounted for senior citizens.

For television match officials: I have secured sponsorship with Specsavers so you can avoid decisions that prompt those with normal eyesight to exclaim, 'What the fuck are you doing?'

For the IRB and their elite referees: I'm very sorry, but those who don't keep their promises get nothing.

For that lovely lad Danny Cipriani: a signed DVD of *The Crying Game*.

And a few gifts for general rugby lovers: if you want to steal a march on the rest, I have done a deal with Smugs Tours and secured huge discounts on their exclusive packages, for the knock-out stages only, to the 2011 World Cup in New Zealand. Those of you who know your team will either be winners or at the very least will reach the final should book now to reserve your very own camper van.

If you're sweating over whether you will get a pay rise, I have the EOS card. Backed by the Northern Shock Bank, if you play this card during contract negotiations it will get you a four-year bonus even before the results of your latest sales initiative are known.

I know some of you want your fifteen minutes of fame, and for that I can take you on a short cut to the top of the world as I have secured a number of those incredible 'All Black jerseys'. Modelled closely on the Mithril Mail made in Erebor for a young Elf Prince, from metal found only in Khazad-dum, and worn by Frodo Baggins during the Quest of Mount Doom, the ABJ makes the wearer appear 'world class' yet renders the wearer invisible when worn in France.

A boon for the many driven to distraction by the drivel spouted on television, I have the Com-Zapper. Plug this into your remote control and whenever Butler, Moore, Harrison or Barnes make a mistake, push the red button to deliver a 200-volt shock to their headphones. (Limited to five shocks per game under European Health and Safety regulations.)

And, finally, to Matt Hampson, Ali Johnson, Paul Sutton and all others battling with serious game-related injuries: the best wishes and support of the whole rugby fraternity. Your courage and humour are humbling, and I hope you and your carers have as good a Christmas as you can.

2

Lawrence Dallaglio's tears for a life ending

June 2008

In a time long, long ago, my then club Richmond won the league and gained promotion to what is now the Premiership on the last day of the season. Crowning this was the knowledge that we had beaten Sir John Hall's much-lauded Newcastle team into second place.

A changing room that fizzed with euphoria had one place where the sun did not shine; it was my last ever game. At first, tears came slowly and quietly. I managed to commute these for feigned gladness, trying to mirror my team. However, at the end, I was alone save for Scott Quinnell and all restraint failed. I sobbed uncontrollably.

That which had dominated nearly all waking thoughts, save those of work or family, was now gone. How would I now define myself? With what might it be replaced? What would ever provide the astonishing experiences that rugby had given me?

My feelings were akin to those I have felt at bereavements.

Quinnell put a huge arm around me, kissed me and gave me a few words of compassion that remain treasured; that he had purposely stayed to do this showed notable sensitivity.

I cannot aver that Lawrence Dallaglio felt the same as he lifted the Premiership trophy with Wasps on Saturday at Twickenham. My description is personal; both of circumstance and personality.

All morning I had been thinking about what he was feeling as the seminal moment approached. I thought about sending him a supportive text but decided he had enough to deal with without old gits bothering him. However, I'll bet there was a kernel of all I state in the thoughts and emotions which swept through Dallaglio from the point he left the field.

When he tries to explain them, I think he will find it difficult to discern precise trains of thought. So many things thrust into your head: past players, games won and lost, moments of triumph and despair; all these flash into view, but have to be trodden down because there is a game looming which demands your attention.

As he stood in the tunnel, Dallaglio's eyes welled and this evoked a fraternal lump in my throat because I had an insight into how he felt. A small voice will have been telling him 'This is the last time, boy; never again; all the dreams; all the triumphs; all over.'

It was almost inevitable that the fates would engineer his final game to take place before a world-record crowd for a club game, and on a Saturday with no other major sporting event to employ the thoughts of the sports press. Dallaglio likes a big stage, and he played his part with no concession to advancing age.

The ovation he received from all supporters of a sold-out Twickenham recognised the passing of an extraordinary career. The temporary hatred of rival factions – for it has almost come to that – was put aside for a wonderful minute.

That moment will have registered with Dallaglio as it occurred, but his side still had a game to win. Thus, the emotion that showed on his face was restrained in deference to a wider cause. He will have been rightly content at the bestowed honour, but the significance thereof will not register properly until he has time for reflection. Tears will have been shed later because he is a passionate man. However, these will not be the tears of shame, or failure, just genuine emotion and regret for a life ending.

In his past games, many will not have understood his vast

contribution to his sides' success. Everyone sees who makes the yards when driving forward. Fewer spot the thorough nuisance Dallaglio made of himself while around the loose ball. With consummate skill, he slowed the ball down sufficiently to allow his colleagues to organise effective defence. With his power, he was often the core of driving mauls that battered opponents. He was a brilliant organiser of his team and any pack in which he played; and, as an aside, a ready and willing adviser to referees. Many accused him of illegality and they have a point, but most of the time he pushed to the limit what referees would allow.

Today's players are given advice about retirement, what it will bring and what it takes away. This is an important function of the Professional Players' Association because the psychological effects of retirement are real, however much the ignorant in the press or in the bar dismiss such a notion as imported American rubbish.

Most people have to face retirement, but this comes at the end of their working life. They have built up to this moment and they do not intend to work again. This is different for a sportsman. He has to deal with the thought that when only half his life is over he has had to give up that at which he excelled and that nothing will equal the myriad experiences he has had. Now he has to work like everyone else, do the mundane things like commuting; the only surprise to me is that more sportsmen do not sink into addiction in an attempt to recreate the intensity of what they felt.

Dallaglio is now taking his coaching exams and plans to continue in the game through that medium. I have no doubt he will succeed, but whatever a player says there is nothing like playing; not coaching, not managing, not commentating. They may come near, but are mere imitations of the real deal.

Few players are able to bow out with a script as implausible as an amusing Sylvester Stallone film, but Dallaglio has never been ordinary. He may have played as such occasionally, but at all times he has been unlike most men.

3

Wimbledon is so hideously English

June 2008

Unless you are in the retail trade, the two weeks of Wimbledon are a nightmare for residents. It is a myth that we locals rent out our homes for thousands, and thus I cannot escape. In defence of this whinge, I hated Wimbledon before I lived there.

For two weeks the country slips into collective madness akin to that surrounding a royal wedding. Wimbledon deftly combines traits of the English that I abhor.

Take queuing for the limited number of tickets that are not in the hands of the corporates and without any complaint.

I would give the fanatics some credit if they vented their spleen at having to drink Chef's Square-Shaped Soups for four days when interviewed; but, no, it's always 'Could be worse', or 'It's not that bad once your limbs go numb' (to match their brains, presumably).

Unbelievably, some of these people watch only a fraction of the day's play, before getting back in the queue for the next day. At least the campers don't need to pay the usurious prices. I am used to rip-off 'London charging', but so expensive was the quote for strawberries last year, nearly 25p for each little fruit, I suggested they might consider selling them individually.

And never have so many bottles of metallic NV champagne been bought without anyone realising a decent Cava would be better.

There are lots of punters from the City so at least this means they drink rather than watch the tennis. Thus, there are fewer people to indulge in another hideous English trait: cheering for losers.

If any League One football team's supporters had had to wait as long as this English crowd for glory, they would have been vandalising the fibreglass wagon wheels on the gates of the chairman's house.

Not only do we indulge losing, we are so terribly nice about it. The legendary NFL coach Vince Lombardi summed it up: 'Show me a good loser and I'll show you a loser.'

Finally, whether the All England Club likes or accepts this, tennis is middle, if not upper, class. The numbers playing are dismally low and not of the demographic that makes athletes strain for success as a way to a better life.

I don't care how many youth initiatives are launched, or how much is given to the Lawn Tennis Association – the image of the game will not change until the All England Club changes. Yes, they let local kids play on the courts as part of a scheme, but none of them will be able to join the Club.

Perception is set from the top down. When I went to join a local club, I was told that I would have to attend their club nights first. This was for two reasons: 'to see what standard I was' (actually, I am probably a reasonable club second teamer, but I thought: how do you start if you have not played before?); also 'to see what sort of a person I was'. I left immediately.

If you want to join the big one, it's even worse. The lame excuse for not expanding the membership of the All England is even given on their website: membership has to be limited because with it comes the right to tickets for the Championships. If they had more members, they would have to give away more tickets. Why can't they simply create another class of membership, which does not have such rights? What they really mean is they are determined to keep the club exclusive.

Before this is dismissed as a chippy rant, how many English players in the world rankings are in the top 100?

4

Sepp Blatter needs a lesson in history

July 2008

In the eighteenth century slaves were transported in ships so tightly packed that dehydration, dysentery and scurvy led to the death of one in three. Slaves who were thought not to be working hard enough suffered arbitrary punishment; in the worst cases – for theft, disloyalty and the like – methods designed to give the maximum pain to the victim were used. The gibbet, for a slow and painful death by hanging; flogging to death; the use of the wheel; and hanging, drawing and quartering (where the person being hanged was cut while still alive).

Eschewing the comparison of older conditions for slaves, let us look at the definition of modern-day slavery. This is defined as the submission to authority for the purpose of subsistence; contract slaves are described as generally poor, often illiterate, and people who are tricked into signing contracts they do not understand.

Signal the obligatory comment from Herr Sepp Blatter. Blatter has long been willing to pontificate on all things English, usually to interfere or warn England that they risk censure for any manner of things. Strangely, he shows no similar regard for other countries; Spain, for example. While worthy European champions, they were lucky to be in the finals following the racist behaviour of their fans towards black players only a few years previously. From Herr Blatter what did we hear on this? Platitudes, but no effective action; talk, talk, talk.

When questioned about Cristiano Ronaldo's apparent desire to break his contract with Manchester United in order to join Real Madrid, Blatter said: 'The important thing is we should also protect the player. If the player wants to play somewhere else, then a solution should be found, because if he stays in a club where he does not feel comfortable, then it's not good for the player or the club. I'm always in favour of protecting the player and if the player, he wants to leave, let him leave. I think in football there's too much modern slavery in transferring players or buying players, and putting them somewhere. We are trying to intervene in such cases. The reaction to the Bosman law is to make long-lasting contracts in order to keep the players and then if he wants to leave, then there is only one solution, he has to pay his contract.'

Herr Blatter must either have a tenuous grasp of history, or be unforgivably insensitive to use the word 'slavery' in relation to the allegedly unfair treatment of Ronaldo. The fact that Ronaldo has agreed with Blatter's words shows what a preening, pampered Portuguese pillock he is. None of the modern-day definitions of slavery apply. I know not whether he is literate, or stupid, but he employs professionals to advise him and cannot be said not to have understood the legal obligations he undertook when his advisers negotiated a lucrative five-year contract with United, presumably with his full knowledge and permission.

As a trained lawyer, Blatter obviously has no problem saying the first thing that comes to mind to support his case, even if it appears contrary to what he has said previously. He must think we are all thick and suffer from amnesia.

It was only in January 2008 that Blatter and FIFA reacted angrily to a ruling by the Court of Arbitration for Sport on the Andy Webster case.

Earlier, on 4 April 2007, the FIFA dispute resolution chamber found Webster guilty of having breached his employment contract without just cause, outside the protected period. Webster wanted to leave his club, Heart of Midlothian, to play for Wigan Athletic.

As a consequence, FIFA ordered him to pay Hearts compensation of £625,000.

The CAS reduced the payment to £150,000, which was the value of the remaining period of the contract. Thus, there was no punitive element. The decision implies that the amount of compensation to be paid by a player who terminates his contract prematurely without just cause after the protected period can easily be calculated in advance; further than that, there is no element of penalty to be included.

Many commentators agreed with the opinion that the ruling would be detrimental to the system but probably advantageous for players' agents, who, as in Webster's case, will offer their clients to new clubs with a price tag on them. Small clubs that are already struggling to keep their squad together, in particular if they have promising players in their team, will be faced with even more aggressive approaches towards their players once the relevant contracts have passed the protected period.

Of this Blatter said: 'The decision which CAS took on 30 January 2008 is very damaging for football and a Pyrrhic victory for those players and their agents, who toy with the idea of rescinding contracts before they have been fulfilled. CAS did not properly take into consideration the specificity of sport as required by article 17, paragraph 1 of the Regulations on the Status and Transfer of Players.

'Because of this unfortunate decision, the principle of contractual stability, as agreed in 2001 with the European Commission as part of the new transfer regulations and which restored order to the transfer system, has been deemed less important than the short-term interests of the player involved.'

Blatter presided over the agreement, in March 2001, of FIFA's transfer regulations, following discussions with all stakeholders – including player and club representatives as well as the European Commission. They are based on the central pillar of maintaining contractual stability between professionals and clubs. Unilateral early termination of a contract between a player and a club without just cause by either party, even if committed after the protected period, still remains an unjustified breach of contract. So which is it, Herr Blatter – which of these contradictory points of view do you maintain?

Come to think of it, if Ronaldo is being treated like a slave, perhaps Sir Alex Ferguson might like to avail himself of one of the punishments listed above. I wonder which of the cruel and unusual ones he would favour.

Meanwhile, FIFA and Herr Blatter remain completely ineffective in combating the issues that weekly bring football into disrepute. Players diving, feigning injury, trying to get others sent off. On these, where is the leadership of Blatter? Why is he not investigating the proper use of technology to assist referees in games? I could go on and on.

Finally, I haven't even started to list the multifarious allegations of a more sinister nature that surround Herr Blatter's presidency. These would take a whole supplement; suffice to say serious allegations remain and have not been conclusively refuted by Herr Blatter or by FIFA.

Should such an important office be held by a person whose grasp of legal decisions appears woefully inept; a person who either does not understand, or does, but does not care, that the use of the word 'slavery' is insulting to the memory of those who suffered, and those who continue to suffer because of that abhorrent system?

The Open: Chris Evert obsession
is not fair game

July 2008

The Open golf was fascinating, though unusual. Congratulations to Pádraig Harrington for a tenacious series of rounds and producing it when it mattered most.

I followed the Open via a number of media platforms and became thoroughly hacked off by some of the coverage.

Further evidence of the obsession with tittle-tattle was the numerous references to Greg Norman's partner, Chris Evert. An appeal to spot her on the Royal Birkdale course, so that 'we can have a word with her', left me in despair. I don't care; she obviously did not want to be interviewed or she would not have tried to hide.

Also, conditions were bad, sometimes very bad, but that is links golf. A morbid preoccupation with the weather produced some risible comments; I particularly liked the Damoclean conundrum one commentator said was facing a player because of his cap. 'Very difficult; he needs his cap to keep warm, but the wind might just lift it at the wrong time.' Well, could he not take it off for the shot and put it back on to walk about? A novel remedy, perhaps; but they are professionals.

Also, we do not want to know how difficult it is to do your job; how cold you are; that your rainwear doesn't fit and so on. Most people, wrongly, think your job is a doss; whining about things only makes them angry, not empathetic. Players made comments that left me thinking they, particularly the Americans, have become a bit nesh.

Conditions were unfair because they gave some players an advantage due to their tee-off time; they did not allow the public to see the brilliance of the professionals; the tournament might be won over par, and Tiger Woods wasn't there. Tee-off times always advantage some; starting in the searing heat of the day in the United States, as opposed to an earlier, cooler time, is a disadvantage. Unless you devise a way to allow all players to start at the same time, that risk remains. Conditions were claimed to be almost, if not actually, unplayable; clearly untrue. Each day players throughout the list scored par, or under, so it was possible.

The public are capable of understanding this. They did not see an exhibition of target golf, often dull anyway, but they saw players in difficulties to which they could relate. There was probably a little *Schadenfreude* at seeing professionals having to cope with the unfamiliarity of multiple bogeys.

As for Tiger not being there – do you think Harrington gives a monkey's?

Finally, shouting 'Get in the hole'. Bad enough in an American accent. With a British one, there are reasonable grounds for summary execution.

John O'Neill threat of rugby doom is bullying

July 2008

Looks like they're getting desperate: the proponents of the experimental law variations (ELVs) are stooping to thinly veiled threats of schism to force their reluctant counterparts into line.

Australian Rugby Union boss John O'Neill has warned that rugby risks being split if northern hemisphere countries do not embrace the ELVs. This follows the refusal of England, Ireland and Wales to trial them.

'You would hate to think we would end up in a situation of two games [but] it could happen,' said O'Neill. 'Over the last few weekends we have seen the Springboks play the All Blacks in two wonderful Test matches and we've seen Australia versus France and Australia versus Ireland and the All Blacks versus England under the old laws. You don't have to be Einstein to figure out which game is a far more impressive spectacle.

'We're simply saying to England, Wales and Ireland – and to the IRB – give it a fair go. To sit back and say "No, we're not trialling them" is not in the best interests of the world game.'

This is just the sort of flawed justification that I have previously highlighted. The Boks v. Blacks Tests were between countries numbered one and two respectively in world rugby; that they were better games than those involving northern hemisphere teams against clearly superior opponents is not surprising.

As for them being an endorsement of the success of the ELVs – rubbish.

This pseudo logic has manifested itself in several other alleged truisms: 'the ball is in play longer', 'more tries are scored', 'coaches think they are a huge step forward'.

All are now parroted without any intellectual scrutiny in the hope that repetition will give them ineluctable truth. Actually, I am grateful to O'Neill because perhaps people will now look properly at all the claims about the ELVs.

When O'Neill says things are not in the best interests of the world game, he really means the Australian game. Only in his country do they have a problem competing with rugby league; why a whole sport's rules should be reorganised to combat this singular threat remains unanswered.

It is perfectly possible for a refusal to enter into this process to be in the best interests of the world game. Not doing something that appears to you to be arrant nonsense is usually called common sense. Under O'Neill's logic it would be wrong to refuse to stick your hand in a fire, because others have done it.

O'Neill and his supporters have not helped themselves by introducing and then dropping so many variations. They have further confused everyone by trialling certain proposed changes in some competitions and not in others. This haphazard approach would never be accepted as a valid form of development in any other context.

For what it's worth, my take on the specific ELVs is that they are fine apart from the following: allowing the maul to be collapsed; allowing any number of players in the line-out; handling on the floor being allowed; awarding free-kicks when the ball is unplayable; drawing an offside line at the tackle; and reducing all offences other than foul play, offside, and repetition/deliberate infringement to free-kicks.

Unfortunately, while the situation continues in this confusing manner, anyone with a modest degree of scepticism about the motives of O'Neill et al. is perfectly right to say *non* until they go away and come back with something which is cogent and not supported by flawed reasoning.

And finally: nobody likes to be bullied or has much respect for someone who takes their bat home. If you want to go your own way, then go; see how far you get without the economic power of England and France. Our game will be the poorer without you, but we will always have one.

Michael Schumacher is just a good old boy

August 2008

A cowboy sporting Stetson and spurs sits astride a magnificent steed. The background is a late medieval moated castle, white-tipped oast houses and rolling English countryside. Last weekend found me in Bodiam, East Sussex, at the Garden of England International Festival of Western Riding.

I have never been into equestrianism. My inverted snobbery does not favour gymkhanas where Bunty competes with Poppy to see who can extort most out of their guilt-ridden yet pushy middle-class parents.

Watching dressage is, to me, akin to putting my testicles on a chopping board with cloves of garlic, to be used by a celebrity chef cooking for five thousand Glaswegian labourers. That this discipline is derived from the evasive actions used by knights during battle makes it no more interesting.

Recovery only seemed likely with a large drink, so I headed to the VIP area. This was cordoned off by a line of four-inch-high wooden sticks that even an asthmatic ant could have scaled.

The VIPs and judges, as was *de rigueur*, were completely kitted out western-style. Country music played gently in the background and I had a sudden, wild, urge to go and request 'Coward of the County' by Kenny Rogers. Get a grip, for God's sake.

Throughout the day things remained reliably strange, Belgians,

Dutch, Americans, all nations riding under the sun for good cash prizes.

Unaccountably, I was drawn to the western riding equivalent of dressage – reining – derived from the skills needed by ranchers to drive cattle across vast plains.

As I watched, my brain again spun when it clocked a stiffly erect Teutonic-looking man, dressed in cowboy jeans, also staring avidly at the riders – Michael Schumacher. I gawped at an iconic world-class sportsman whose concentration was intense.

Should I approach him and elicit fascinating revelations? No, it was enough to watch him watch. His analysis and comment outdid those about him who, I was informed, were experienced enthusiasts, some quite high-level competitors. Perhaps that's why he is the honorary show president.

The charming Honourable Lady Francesca Sternberg reeled off statistics with such rapidity I could barely take them in – then again, her tight cowboy jeans were distracting.

Reining is being pushed as a discipline for riders at the Olympic Games. Its enthusiasts have widely different backgrounds and incomes, all informing me that western riding has numerous adherents. The event was being webcast worldwide.

Ultimately it is the feeling of equality that makes western riding just much more enjoyable than its stuffy English counterparts like the Cartier Polo and Hickstead.

Accuse the attendees of being irredeemably naff and they wouldn't give a damn. They are not there to see and be seen anyway. And Michael Schumacher – he's just another good old boy.

8

Team GB in Beijing – how to
win without petulance

August 2008

The performance of Team GB exceeded the targets set by UK
Sport, whose investment it repaid, and then some. It also proved
that the link between investment and performance is indubitable;
you get what you pay for. As a result, when Team GB arrive back
in Britain they will receive a welcome that will exceed all expectation due to the effect their success has had on the nation.

The British are hungry for sporting triumph because it is so
rare; sport is the last arena in which we can battle Johnny
Foreigner. Although we like a near miss, this is probably a defence
mechanism against decades of disappointment and I defy anyone
not to have found a moment of inspiration from Beijing.

Team GB have just competed in an event large enough for
comparisons to be made with the national game, and football has
been found wanting.

There is growing displeasure at the preternatural wages earned
by our leading footballers, compared with what they give.
Footballers like to say 'Show us your medals' to those from outside who have the temerity to involve themselves in their sport, but
people realise that no current British player can claim to have even
been in the final of football's biggest tournament.

The manner in which our athletes have gone about their business, their respect for officials and the way they have borne

success and failure has been a refreshing change from the snarling petulance of footballers.

Football fans wrongly claim their sport is more passionate and pressured than any other and that, with so much at stake, bad behaviour is inevitable. But was there less passion in, or pressure on, any member of Team GB, who, lest we forget, knew that in this one tournament four years of dedication would be at stake? If they got it wrong it meant four more years of dedication before they could try again.

It has become apparent how much preparation has been necessary for each athlete to maximise his or her chance of winning. Sacrifice is not too strong a word for the restricted lifestyle accepted as the price of success.

Even though FIFA president Sepp Blatter claims slavery exists at Old Trafford, no footballer is close to adopting a similar regime. Why? Because they do not have to.

So craven are football's governing bodies and fans that they accept what is given without enquiring how much better their game and players could be if the latter copied our athletes.

Inevitably, there have been knockers, those who feel it necessary to criticise, as if this is clever. They whinge about the cost of Olympic success and how many hospitals could have been built with the money, but if we took a lead from our athletes and did a modest amount of exercise we would not need as many.

Alternatively, they focus on the term 'elite' – it's a class thing. The word refers to the position reached by the athlete; it has nothing to do with privilege, power or social standing. In any event, there is nothing wrong with elitism, provided it is based on performance and not the things aforementioned. We do not want the lowest common denominator.

The sports of cycling and rowing have been specifically attacked. If there is social elitism in rowing the way to open it out is to encourage existing clubs to widen their membership. Those who say it is elitist do not mention the background of Sir Steven

Redgrave, our greatest Olympian, who went to Great Marlow Comprehensive.

As for cycling, there are few families in Britain that cannot afford a bike. Elite? You're 'avin' a giraffe, mate. The adult sub-scription for membership to British Cycling starts at £13, about the cost of two packets of fags.

They should be criticising the fact that Team GB now find their budget is in jeopardy for London 2012. The much trumpeted public investment of £600 million in sport for 2012 stated that £100 million of this had to be raised by UK Sport. Anyone in sponsorship could have told the Government this was untenable.

First, to raise that much money requires specialised skills, which nobody has within UK Sport. Secondly, UK Sport would strug-gle as London 2012 is also fighting for sponsors for the Games.

The present shortfall of about £79 million, unless guaranteed, will mean UK Sport having to implement fall-back plans whereby each sport will have to revise downwards the plans it made in expectation of receiving the full £600 million.

No athlete will give up his or her present income and go full time with just the hope that funds might be available.

Future governments, whatever their hue, have the legacy of Beijing and the promise of London 2012 which will keep sport in the public's consciousness. It has this unique opportunity to build and invest in sport – a one-off chance finally to silence those who deride sport because it is physical, not cerebral. Those who bear a life-long grudge because they got picked last for any team at school.

What sport needs, and deserves, is its own place at the Cabinet table. This would attract politicians of ability rather than also-rans and would secure its funding long term.

We could then set about reaping the benefits of exercise, self-discipline, sportsmanship, diet and how to work within a team; learning how to cope with winning and losing; and providing meaningful alternatives to indolence and petty crime.

BBC Olympic coverage is value for money

August 2008

'£3m of licence payers' money'; 'More staff sent than athletes' –
so claimed those parts of the press that hate the BBC, in particular, the *Daily Mail*.

When a paper wishes to illustrate unwarranted largesse, a total
figure is highlighted; when the reverse (e.g. the cost of the Civil
List), they use a cost per head to the GB population.

Well, using their method of calculation and their claimed figures, this element of the BBC's provision over sixteen days of
2,750 hours of TV, radio online, six interactive streams, mobiles
online and the World Service, has cost each of us £0.05.

If the stunning successes of Team GB had been pay-per-view
(and bear in mind you would never get sixteen days of events for
one fee anyway) at, say, £14.99, we would have paid almost 6,814
times more.

The BBC should get stick when it is deserved, but this is not
such an occasion.

London must match Sydney's support of Paralympics

August 2008

The year before the 2000 Olympics I was in Sydney watching a rugby league State of Origin game. At half-time there was the final qualifier for the disabled men's 100 metres, the prize being a place in the Paralympic team for the Sydney Games.

What surprised me, apart from how fast the race was run, was that nearly all the crowd stayed to watch. My Aussie mate told me this was usual. He said that, following the main Sydney Games, there would be the same number of volunteers and crowds would be very good. I admit I was more than sceptical.

It turned out that he was right and I was wrong. The Sydney Paralympic athletics saw the Olympic Stadium full, with 110,000 spectators.

What will the response of the Chinese be to the next two weeks? Well, it is probably not a fair test, as they are able to compel volunteers and spectators, but it cannot be as bad as Atlanta 1996, when most Americans tried to pretend it wasn't happening.

The Paralympics are worth watching, not out of patronising sympathy for how well the athletes have coped with their disability, but for their sporting prowess itself. For each Paralympian, the same sacrifice and dedication is demanded as from their able-bodied equivalent.

I believe the support given to the Paralympics by the host nation says much about both its humanity and whether it has an intrinsic love of sport. I only hope London 2012 will replicate Sydney and not Atlanta.

Time for the Olympic carping team to put up or shut up

August 2008

We couldn't even have a nanosecond of basking in the Beijing triumphs before the moaning started on the phone-ins. The non-London synchronised carping team swung into action, complaining about their lack of representation during the Beijing parades, in the London segment of the closing ceremony, or in London 2012 itself.

I thought the eight-minute slot filled by Beckham et al. was toe-curling – not because it didn't have anyone in a kilt, flat cap or any whippets; it was just naff.

It doesn't matter that no other city in Britain could have won the bid to host the Games; these bitter people would rather no one had them than they go to what they think is an already overmighty monstrosity.

Although, for example, research undertaken by both the Yorkshire and Humberside and East of England Development Agencies estimates that each could benefit by £600 milllion from London 2012, this still hasn't stopped the claim that London alone will benefit economically. As a net contributor to GDP, London already subsidizes the rest of Britain. No matter, the rest want their piece of the pie. That is, they want the pie, but don't want to pay for it. A direct quote from one caller typified the thrust of these whingers: 'It's London's Games; let Londoners pay for it.'

As a London resident, I and fellow Londoners, on top of the above, will pay a large premium in council tax for London 2012. I'm happy to do so, but not if all I get from elsewhere is bleating. I presume the said caller would agree that seeing as London residents will, as he wishes, pay for the Games, tickets should be restricted to those with London postcodes.

One youth worker could not wait to play the race card: what is it going to do for the average coloured youth? Nothing, if they sit on their backsides, determined not to be involved.

Anyone who strives can reach the sky, like Christine Ohuruogu and Phillips Idowu; then again, that would mean taking responsibility for your own advancement and lots of hard work.

Obviously, gold medals cannot be won by everybody, but the discipline involved in trying would lift any youth, of any race, at least away from a life of torpor and leave a belief that they can achieve elsewhere.

As for the Celtic fringe of the carping team, could it get any sillier?

Stewart Maxwell, the Scottish Minister for Sport, wants Scotland to have its own Olympic team. Well, we wouldn't have been competing under the GB banner had it not been thought up by a Scotsman and had the Scots not accepted just short of £400,000, plus £20,000 in bribes, to sign the Treaty of Union in 1707.

While attempting to make his isolationist fantasy real, he might speak to Chris Hoy, Scotland's fantastic Olympian, who identified the flaw in his argument. There is no national infrastructure capable of supporting Scottish athletes. That is why they have relocated to England.

One Welsh windbag complained that Welsh athletes were not allowed to wave the Welsh flag, nor was there anything Welsh in the eight-minute slot. Could I point out that London isn't in Wales and the English members of Team GB, who won the vast majority of medals, didn't get to parade the flag of St George, but didn't complain and were happy to share the stage with their Celtic team-mates?

Look, if you don't want to be involved – fine; but just shut up and leave those of us who are proud to host the world's athletes to get on with it in peace.

Andriy Shevchenko's Chelsea figures don't add up

August 2008

It's a good job Chelsea don't have to reveal the loan details paid by AC Milan for the return of one of their most prolific goalscorers, Andriy Shevchenko. The lack of transfer fee speaks volumes about just how bad a piece of business was his acquisition, rivalled only by that of Winston Bogarde in 2000.

Some £30 million and £120,000 per week got Chelsea nine league goals and a player who became, unwittingly or not, a divisive presence in the dressing room. It was not just that he was not doing what he had been bought to do but that he was seen to have the favour of Roman Abramovich.

There is always antipathy towards the teacher's pet. Although he may not always have deserved this moniker, Shevchenko's translation of Abramovich's tactical advice to Michael Essien after one game solidified his image as far as the rest of the Chelsea squad were concerned.

Shevchenko has said that he thanks the fans for their support while at Chelsea; I should think so. The full opprobrium he deserved was withheld for two reasons; he at least looked as if he was trying, and there was respect for his undoubted former brilliance. The nearest he got to public vilification was the chant 'You're so shit, that you let Sheva score.'

If anyone is to blame for Carlos Tévez debacle, it is the Premier League

September 2008

One of the first comments that will be made on the ruling of the independent tribunal in the matter of Sheffield United against West Ham United will be that it was not that of a court. Maybe, but this will not wash because the panel are all highly qualified legally and both parties nominated one of the panel. This jurisdiction was mandated under Football Association rules and there is no right of appeal. That does not mean it is impossible to appeal, but the process is tortuous and legally difficult. West Ham, against whom the panel ruled, are now in a very difficult position.

There are some who question why this case was allowed to be brought at all, given that the question of playing the ineligible Tévez was dealt with by the Premier League and West Ham fined £5.5 million.

Unfortunately, unless it is clearly frivolous or vexatious, a court or tribunal cannot throw out even an unlikely case, unless they find evidence from which they can conclude that it has no prospects of success, even if the factual matrix (list of actual facts pertaining to a case) averred by the party seeking damages is accepted.

What this tribunal had to decide was this: had it not been for Tévez, would West Ham have won enough points to stay up?

Much was made of Tévez's contributions to the West Ham win

over Manchester United at Old Trafford, but they would also have considered the fact that Tévez had scored six goals in West Ham's previous nine games. The tribunal decided they would not, and the damages flowing therefrom will be the subject of a further hearing.

The point has been forcefully made by many in the football world – in and out of the media – that nobody is able to know what the results would have been had Tévez not played following his ineligible registration. The debate over this sort of issue sinks quickly into philosophical realms. The tribunal decision would not have passed the first meditation of Descartes and his basic strategy of considering false any belief that falls prey to the slightest doubt. This 'hyperbolic doubt' is summoned to criticise what is labelled a 'guess' by the tribunal.

The emotions that surround this matter are strong and cloud the real issues; the element of 'morality', in itself a hugely questionable concept, is with Sheffield. They went down and suffered all that that entails. Their most direct rival played an ineligible player and stayed up.

Though the decision of the tribunal, indeed of any ruling body, is open to question, that does not in itself make it wrong, whatever the father of modern philosophy states. If these bodies did not indulge in this kind of speculation there would be no civil jurisdiction within which claims could be decided. You may not like this, but it is the foundation of the civil legal system and is used to decide cases infinitely more complex – and could I cause controversy by saying with more importance? – than the one at issue.

Those who criticise the ruling by using the claim that it is no more than crystal-ball gazing are stating a truism. Moreover, one that is rejected by all litigants who accept the strictures faced by the body from which they seek the ruling.

Those who speculate about what would have happened had former Sheffield United player Steve Kabba played for Watford against his old team, in United's only win of their last five matches that season, are missing the point. That was not an issue over which this tribunal was asked to rule. If it had been, for example in a pleading from the respondent, then it would have been dealt with in the same way, on the balance of probabilities.

The precedent set is not a welcome one, but the alternative is to say that there is no right of redress at all in matters which involve calculated estimation of fact and consequence, i.e. anything at all. Decisions are made with some regard to the precedent they may set, but this is not and should not be the deciding factor in the decision to be made at that time. What others decide to do as a consequence involves as much speculation as that decried in the judgement in which the precedent is created. How do you know that it will lead to a flood of challenges to all manner of football issues?

Finally, I question whether West Ham were the cause of any damage suffered, given that the eligibility issue had been ruled upon and they had been fined by the Premier League. Once that decision had been made I believe they were entitled to consider the ineligibility issue closed.

Whether they should have had points docked and not a fine is a different argument, but not one which Sheffield United thought important enough to launch legal action at the time. If anybody caused this damage it was the Premier League, who allowed West Ham to continue fielding Tévez.

14

England need more than pride and passion to create winning mentality

September 2008

Passion and pride are two things that Fabio Capello is said to have restored to England's football team. If this is so, he should not have had to; these are rudiments for any international player. Moreover, though they contribute, they do not win games.

England's impressive 4–1 win that ended Croatia's long, unbeaten home record was achieved because of the discipline shown in executing a game plan; each player doing the job demanded, not gallivanting about through frustration or inattentiveness. The game plan initiated by Capello differentiates him from the last two England managers – you could see what it was and it worked. Though it was an impressive performance, remember what happened after the 5–1 thrashing of Germany. There are still many things that need attention.

The term world class is appended to many England players but the best measure is that of the players themselves. The FIFPro World XI for the three seasons from 2004 to 2007 shows that only John Terry (three times) and Frank Lampard and Steven Gerrard (once each) have been selected. If England can manage to play as a team this might not matter; Greece 2004 (in the European Championship) is an apposite lesson of the triumph of the unified over the individual.

In seeking team displays, it may be tempting to pick the most talented XI, but this should only be done if they combine.

Though the manager might want both, the Lampard/Gerrard question has to be sorted. The evidence is now overwhelming: for whatever reason, and it matters not what it is, they do not coalesce. Either could do the job, but Capello must choose. At least he has the luxury of knowing he has an experienced replacement if the event of injury or loss of form. In addition, the residence of one of two very good midfielders on the bench will signal the end of nepotism and reintroduce one of the best motivational aids – competition for selection.

Further, Michael Owen, when fit, is more talented than Emile Heskey or Peter Crouch, but the Croatia game showed that a target man who can hold up the ball not only gives the midfield time to get into the box and provides a target for the wingers, but it also helps Wayne Rooney make a full contribution. If a lesser talent heading the attack is the price of Rooney being empowered, it is a price worth paying.

In addition to the tactical and selection issues, there are intangible matters that require solution, because they will contribute to ultimate failure as surely as defects in the aforementioned.

There are common traits in teams that dominate and England's football team need to look closely at these and replicate them if possible.

Terry, the captain, referred to a fear of failure within the camp, especially when England play at Wembley. 'At club level the lads feel free and can express themselves. Once an England game has started, we play the short and easy passes, whereas if I was playing for Chelsea and hit a long pass that didn't come off, the fans would still sing my name.'

I knew this fear when I played; it is real and can be crippling. Fear of failure is fear of not living up to the standards set by illustrious predecessors; fear of losing, of not doing the things needed to give the team victory.

Terry's words do not describe fear of failure, i.e. of losing; they describe a fear of unpopularity, and that is not the same thing. What the fans may, or may not think, or whether they will sing your name, are utterly the wrong yardsticks. Furthermore, such matters are beyond a player's direct control anyway. He must concentrate on the things he can control.

Terry should not fear playing at Wembley; the fans will support effort and skill, but this has been so little in evidence until now that they were entitled to vent their feelings.

Consistency. England have to show Wednesday night's victory was not an anomaly. Great teams cannot always be brilliant, but they fashion wins in adversity and have a standard of performance below which they do not fall. This is professionalism, not how many cars you can buy.

Great teams also cope with the mantle of being favourites; they do not need backs-to-the-wall adversity to elicit extraordinary effort. A bullying mentality is required; not distasteful behaviour, but a lack of compassion that allows a team to hammer the weak.

It also requires that the same concentration, preparation and effort is attended on the opposition, whoever they are. To this must be added constant and candid introspection over the team's standards. Capello may well appreciate these things, but can he carry a group of players who hitherto have demonstrated they are too often recalcitrant?

The England football team also needs a good sports psychologist. I can hear the snorts of derision but, in response, I point out, as did my colleague Alison Kervin earlier this week, that Team GB Cycling's sports psychologist has been in situ for the last seven years. You see if any of the cyclists think that his expertise is gibberish.

FA are hamstrung when it comes to imposing discipline on football

October 2008

'Why don't they do something?' How often have you heard this said, in relation to, well, almost anything? The homogeneous call for action, from, well, almost anyone.

Football – where the calls for someone to get a grip of misbehaviour grow ever louder – is no different, but the three governing bodies covering English football are huge organisations and their statutes and rules voluminous.

While not of the same magnitude as their political counterparts, the regulations and the complexity of the documents might be a cure for insomnia. A simplistic analogy is that of government, regional assembly and local authority: each has its own powers, subject to the framework set by the higher body. While many see the FA as rulers of English football, this is true only in specific areas.

FIFA's statutory power is contractually enshrined in their conditions of membership, UEFA are bound by these, and so, in turn, are the FA. The *de facto* Prime Minister, Sepp Blatter, sits atop FIFA, in spite of allegations – which he has firmly denied – of corruption and nefariousness. Were he merely the titular head this would matter less, but he exercises power both through suggestion and the rules of FIFA, which allow delegated authority from the executive on any issue it divests to him.

As we know, the football world of Herr Blatter is one in which slavery still exists, with players eking out a living on £90,000 per week; where alleged passion excuses vile dissent towards officials and racism is punished by a nominal fine only.

When fans rail at deficiencies within football they should first look at the person leading their game worldwide; it is tempting to dismiss him as a buffoon, but the English, especially the Premier League, need to be aware of Blatter's political effectiveness. In affiliation with Michel Platini, Blatter may soon persuade the EU to allow UEFA the power to run English football in the same way that the EU (Germany and France) run Westminster.

FIFA alone changes the playing rules of football; thus the sensible introduction of technology and so on is not within the gift of the FA; petitioning for change is needed and is long and tortuous.

Each level of football government has control of the tournaments it organises: FIFA have the World Cup; UEFA the Champions League, UEFA Cup and European Championship; the FA have the FA Cup and England internationals. This is important, not just for administrative reasons, but for the income generated by the multifarious sporting rights. This is what underlies club versus country versus hemisphere tensions.

It is important to understand how the FA, especially the twelve-man main board, is constituted. You would think it was the equivalent of rugby's fifty-seven 'old farts', but not so. The Premier and Football Leagues have equal representation, with another six members appointed to speak for the interests of non-professional football, even though the latter accounts for the very substantial majority of those involved in English football.

So when you hear managers, chairmen and fans of professional clubs damning the FA, they should be asked why they are not criticising their own representatives who have an equal say in what is done.

Similarly, in the area of refereeing competence, the FA, Premier League and Football League are all represented on the

Professional Game Match Officials – the body which administers officials operating at the highest levels of domestic football.

If Sir Alex Ferguson believes referees are biased against Manchester United (evidenced by the astounding number of penalties given to opponents at Old Trafford), he should be shouting at his own league first.

The FA compliance department deals with matters relating to breaches of FA rules and regulations, both on the field and off, and any subsequent suspensions of players, from the Premier League to Step 4 of the National League System. However, though it conducts investigations and decides whether charges should be brought, the cases are determined by independent disciplinary commissions. This independence is crucial to avoid allegations of partiality, but it also means decisions have to be accepted, even if they are daft; in fact, no different from ordinary courts.

In the areas of corporate governance, and particularly regulation of agents and club ownership, the FA have the power to investigate and discipline, but again, remember that, in reality, FA also means the leagues themselves.

The 'fit and proper' person test for club ownership is a case of 'to each, his own' – thus the Premier and Football Leagues investigate themselves.

Though, on paper, the regulations seem clear, one wonders how Thaksin Shinawatra, a man about whose human rights record Amnesty International has expressed concern, passed the test. Further, does his successor in ownership of Manchester City, effectively an arm of the nation state of Abu Dhabi, qualify as a person at all?

This leads to the system used to adjudicate on disputes. Through FIFA and UEFA, the FA and their members are bound to use internal arbitration and are specifically excluded from using the courts, other than the Court of Arbitration for Sport – the equivalent of the House of Lords or European Court. It uses FIFA regulations and Swiss law. If you don't like the decisions of independent tribunals you can appeal to, er, an independent tribunal.

Finally, Respect – the £200 million FA initiative to raise standards of behaviour of players, managers, fans, parents, et al. The control of such standards is within the sole province of the FA and is supported by FIFA and UEFA rules.

Will it work? Who knows? It certainly won't work as well as booking all Premier League players who utter dissent, sending off those with two yellows. And if teams end games with seven or eight players, tell the whingers, 'Tough, this is the way it is going to be – get in line or get out', thereafter deducting three points from any team that racks up ten bookings for dissent.

See how quickly managers whose jobs are thus threatened beat their miscreants into line. A hell of a lot cheaper and more effective and, as it is a reform from top down, guaranteed to reach the parts other sanctions might not reach.

16

England's Rugby Union Star Danny Cipriani should stay clear of celebrity world

October 2008

Although apropos of rugby and Danny Cipriani, what follows could apply to any young sports person, in the mad, mad, mad, mad world of celebrity.

Last week, on the BBC's *Inside Sport* programme, the matter of Cipriani and celebrity came up. My basic premise was that, having lived in Soho for six years and having indulged at the then celebrity bars, clubs and events, for all the initial excitement, the world of celebrity is generally vacuous.

In particular, the near-deification of people who are famous for being well known means that ultimately Cipriani will find nothing of long-term satisfaction and it would be wise for him to steer clear as far as he could.

I was lucky. I had retired and was recognised just enough to help me get past door staff, but not so much as to attract much attention. This enabled me to see and sometimes to be part of all manner of outrageous behaviour, most of which would have been front-page fodder for any tabloid.

I don't think the above is even arguable; there is nothing in that world which can make Cipriani a better player. For a professional sportsman that should be the end of the argument.

It is inconceivable that Cipriani will arrive at this conclusion at his age without strong external guidance. This is not being patronising; merely recognising the incredible lure of celebrity. His relationship with an agent is crucial, because it is through good agents that people avoid pitfalls; much more important than the latest, even biggest, commercial deal. A sufficiently experienced figure advises how to stay off the front pages and about even seemingly innocuous remarks that may have unwelcome consequences.

As if to make this very point, a clip was then played wherein Cipriani named me as an example of a former player decrying the behaviour of modern players when I had probably done the same things. 'It shows how people can turn.'

Cipriani's mentors should consider this: if he had really offended me and I was spiteful (he didn't and I am trying to get better on the other) I could abuse my position as a national columnist to subtly criticise Cipriani whenever possible; to whisper to highly placed rugby people about this and that; write up his rivals and so on. I won't do this because from what I see and hear he is actually a decent lad and England need his talent.

Had he made remarks about a scandal columnist, they would not have rested until they shafted him and they wouldn't – ask Lawrence Dallaglio – be above setting him up.

The less I see of Cipriani, other than in the sports sections, the happier and less bored I will be and I suspect all England rugby fans concur.

17

It took courage for the parents of Daniel James to say goodbye

October 2008

The best consequence of success in sport is the opportunity to enrich the life of someone else. This is a feeling nobody, however rich, can buy. As a former international hooker, I know that it also brings other things – equally moving, of greater import and sometimes inspirational, but never a pleasure.

I vividly recall my first visit to a rugby player who was in one of the country's acute centres having suffered serious spinal injury. As I write I can feel the tears welling up and, as then, I cannot stop them.

I was not prepared for the experience, not understanding what might be my reaction. More importantly, what it needed to be to help the unfortunate boy who, either side of a collapsed scrum, had looked forward to his degree course at university, but now contemplated a lifetime of manual evacuation of his bowels, assisted feeding and knowing he would never be independent.

Though rugby is not the most dangerous of sports, there are serious injuries, and those pertaining to the front row, particularly to hookers, resonate keenly. The uniquely vulnerable world of the hooker within the scrum is one in which I dwelt for years without serious injury.

However, I also remember the times I got the engagement, the 'hit', wrong, suffering a 'stinger', a neurological shock like a lightning bolt down my spine: when I was driven upwards, my neck being slowly bent, close to hyperextension, before I managed to pop my head out of the scrum; when the front rows collapsed and all I could do was turn my head a little to minimise the chance of my neck taking all the weight of the collapse and fracturing.

Daniel James, son of Julie and Mark, represented England at Under-16, university and student level as hooker. In playing for the last two teams he was following the same path which years earlier had led me to that which also cannot be bought: the honour of representing your country at full international level.

I know how Daniel felt pulling on the No. 2 jersey; the mixture of fierce determination and pride, edged with fear and the pressure of carrying not only his dreams, but those of his friends and especially his parents. I know Julie and Mark were so very proud.

I am sure that in a quiet moment before he played he thought of his mother and father. How much he owed them for driving him to training, coping with his mood swings according to how he had played – and just how much he loved them. I hope he told them at the time, because too few of us do.

Unfortunately, I know exactly how, in March last year, Daniel dislocated his spine when a scrum collapsed during a training session at Nuneaton RFC.

Colleague Mick Cleary, in his earlier column, chose precisely the phrase which is more apposite to me than most, given the similarities with Daniel.

'There but for . . .'

I cannot dwell on that collapse as it reminds me too much of my mortality and that someone else was chosen by fate to suffer. I cannot know the workings of Daniel's mind as he struggled with his catastrophic injury and, if I am honest, I do not want to because in those thoughts lies madness.

I can make an educated guess at how his mum and dad felt when they were told of his accident and with what they battled thereafter. If the following sounds patronising, so be it; only a parent can come remotely near understanding what it must have been like for Julie and Mark.

If you have not had a child, your perception of this is intellectual. That is what makes parenthood special: it is emotional. You may hypothesise that Julie and Mark would gladly have swapped places with their son; but you cannot feel that or the guilt they probably feel for encouraging him to play the game that, at times, they will feel killed their son.

All this is secondary to the astonishing courage they showed in accompanying Daniel to the Dignitas clinic in Berne, where Daniel was assisted to take a life which to him had become unbearable, particularly given the contradiction of rude health and near-total incapacity.

I do not know how they faced the conflicting emotions of saying goodbye to the little boy they saw score his first try and the desperate wish to keep him with them. If they get counselling, which they must, they may have to face admitting something I felt while watching my father struggle through the last hours of his life, gasping for breath – that when I cried 'Please don't struggle any more', part of this was because I selfishly wanted him to spare me any more pain.

My father was elderly, but still the walk from his deathbed was a searing experience. No parent should have to bury a child and I do not have the ability to suppose what that walk felt like for Julie and Mark.

It is still an offence under the Suicide Act 1961 to 'aid, counsel or procure the suicide of another'; the penalty is up to fourteen years' imprisonment. Julie and Mark now face the ordeal of investigation by the West Mercia Police following notification of their act of love by a 'concerned' individual.

Of that person I say concerned is the last thing you were, other than in an intellectual exercise of morality, a concept incapable of standard definition by two people, never mind entire organised groups – however concerned they, in their delusion, may be.

Among the many letters Julie and Mark will get, there will be a handful which will say they will be punished on the final day. Yes, some people are that pitiful. To such authors I put this – if you reserve judgement for God, why usurp this by presupposing the conclusion?

If there is a God I believe He will understand what was done and why.

Headlines have stated that Julie and Mark have defended their actions. Mr and Mrs James, you have to do no such thing. If there is a final reckoning, it is between you and your God – no one else.

18

Reflections and the effects of the Daniel James article

May 2010

I cannot speak for other writers, but I rarely think that anything I produce is much good, and never, not even with the article which was the subject of the previous chapter, do I step away from my desk thinking that a piece is special. Part of this is constitutional, but some is down to the fact that every writer believes there is a perfect way to tell a story or to pen a phrase, and because any point can be put in so many ways a writer is always aware that his or hers may not be the optimum.

I did think for the previous piece that I had done my best and that the article was strong but the reaction to it genuinely shocked me. I had formerly held the view that, while some sports writers were undoubtedly held in high regard – Martin Samuel, Hugh McIlvanney and Paul Hayward being three of the most noteworthy – even the respect they had earned over a number of years served only to ensure their pieces were read more soberly and given the benefit of thought before reaction. I doubted whether anything written by way of comment could produce much beyond this. I certainly did not believe it was possible to move people to tears or to make any real difference to readers not intimately acquainted with the subject matter at hand.

I knew that there would be a resonance for a number of readers who had played in the front row and who must, by definition, have faced the sort of dangers that can occur when things go wrong; indeed, it was my absolute familiarity with so many aspects of Daniel's career that provided the insight for my comments. Beyond that, I hoped I could provide a little understanding of those dangers and give an impression of why the story had affected me so deeply that at times, while I wrote, I did so through bouts of tears and with a sense of responsibility that made me revisit my copy many times before I had a version with which I was even half satisfied. The extent and nature of the reaction to the article made me see the way in which a newspaper columnist can still cause emotional and thought-provoking reactions to a topic. They also made me realise that such influence should bring about reflection and a determination not to use it for petty or personal reasons, even though I accept that this is sometimes done.

The first thing to say about the many reader comments is that, in the main, they were not the hasty and ill-considered responses often sent as a result of the online comment facility. It is apparent that the authors had taken time to consider the issues and had come to their own conclusions. The articulacy of some of them is such that I believe their words should be read together with mine as they are a powerful addition, and though it takes a bit of time to read them all, the reward more than compensates. When the article appeared online, I was not best pleased that the comment facility was not available until the afternoon, but this turned out to be one of the reasons for the piece penetrating beyond the usual sporting readership.

Sometimes people contact my sports editor rather than/as well as making a comment online. As no facility was available in the sports section, scores of readers sent their comments to the editor-in-chief whose increasingly agitated secretary then passed them on to me, and at one point she asked just what it was I had written and went away to read it for herself. The link for the comments is http://www.telegraph.co.uk/sport/rugbyunion/3242030/It-took-courage-for-the-parents-of-Daniel-James-to-say-goodbye-Rugby-Union.html and it is worth reading them in full for their extraordinary compassion and expressiveness.

The first comments came from rugby followers, then sports readers, and it appears that they recommended it to their non-sporting friends; a few hours later, comments began to come in from readers abroad. Added to these, I had a number posted via my own website and from people who had my e-mail address. They tumbled in and were in the main complimentary; this was very humbling, and in one way I felt guilty because I had exploited a story of pain and hurt and was now receiving praise.

The posts that were critical of my stance divided into two main points: that it was for God and not man to decide about the life of a person; and that I was effectively saying that those who chose not to take the same decision as Daniel and his parents were less brave and in some way inferior. The former criticism is covered in the article: it might be for God to judge, in which case He will do so, but it is not for anybody else to define His will and make that judgement for Him. The latter criticism misunderstands me entirely: it was never my intention to pass such a moral judgement and nor do I think the article can be read that way without pre-conceived notions on the part of a particular reader. The essence of my argument was that such decisions are for those directly involved and are not the business of anyone else. If another person chooses to carry on with life as a tetraplegic then I respect that choice, but it is no more or less brave than what happened with the James family.

As soon as the piece was published I wanted to contact Mark and Julie because I wished to explain my motives behind writing the article and to ask them to forgive my use of their situation for a newspaper column. I did not do this because I was not sure of their reaction, and had it not been positive I had no desire to intrude further into their difficulties. However, shortly after the publication, Radio 5 Live wanted to do a special programme focusing on the Jameses and I was asked to do the interview.

I met Julie and Mark in a Harvester pub the night before the interview because I did not think that they or I would be in the right frame of mind to meet on the day and then launch straight into an interview about this most personal of topics. I was very nervous before the meeting as I was aware that I had brought a fresh bout of media attention on the Jameses and that, while it had been overwhelmingly supportive, it was not me who had to deal with any fallout. What some people fail to understand is that sometimes, at moments of acute grief, any attention, good or bad, feels oppressive.

They were what I knew they would be: a decent couple who had provided all the love and support to their family that they were able to give. They were entirely normal and that does not carry any derogatory insinuations; rather, it puts into sharp focus how an ordinary family can be faced with an extraordinary dilemma. When I asked for their forgiveness for making use of their story, they looked puzzled and asked why I thought I needed this.

Over the next couple of hours they told me their story in great detail and it shocked me. When Daniel was admitted to hospital he still had the use of both arms. However, over the next few agonising hours he was manually turned twice for X-rays. When the Jameses asked about a move to a specialist unit they were told that this would complicate things. They later discovered that Stoke Mandeville had a spare bed that night, but by the time Daniel was transferred a few days later he had lost the use of his arms.

Both Julie and Mark expressed their guilt for not standing up to the doctors and insisting they call the acute centres and demand a place for Daniel. Like many ordinary people they had absolute faith in the doctors and they were not the sort of people to complain, even when they saw Daniel's condition deteriorating.

For the purpose of my original article it was better that I did not know these details because even though they were not relevant to the core subjects of the piece, which were personal choice, parenting and personal courage, it would have been almost impossible to ignore the mistakes, and the article would have been of a different tenor and therefore less powerful.

I was also unaware that Daniel had made two previous and unsuccessful attempts to commit suicide. When they explained to me that Daniel had told them he didn't want to live like this, I realised that I had not appreciated the true nature of the decision they made regarding their son's life and death. It was not a question of them assuming responsibility for his life or death. What they had to decide was whether they would, against all their natural instincts, help their son to die in a dignified way; or whether they would say to him that he must die alone, possibly in pain for several hours, and all because they morally could not countenance assisting the ending of another human being's life.

Julie's interview was broadcast on Radio 5 Live and it brought an extraordinary amount of comment, nearly all of it expressing sympathy and admiration. It is always difficult to balance the need for privacy against the editorial desire to get the best and most emotional story; at the end of the day I think you just have to go with your instincts and respect the boundaries of the person being interviewed. In speaking so openly, Julie was again very brave, speaking softly and eloquently, describing the last hours of her son's life.

I have tried to explain why my reactions to this story were so marked and, although I cannot speak for other people who choose to record their own thoughts, I am sure it was the recognition by many a parent of the nearly impossible dilemma faced by the James family as well as sheer human decency that was behind many of the equally strong comments. Even people who may have come to an alternative conclusion about the decision made by the Jameses mostly still recognised that, in situations like this, nothing can be stated as a certainty; and also that individuals have the right to make choices without the censure of others who, while taking an opposing view, cannot possibly know what they would do if placed in similar circumstances.

I have made no further contact with the James family because I do not feel it is my right to trespass more without invitation. The James family deserves the right to grieve and to recover in private, and all I want to add is that I hope they will come to an accommodation with their feelings. They, as a whole family, have been astonishingly courageous and I know that my best wishes are supplemented by thousands of others.

19

Players' attitudes make the Respect campaign a joke

November 2008

Respect is defined as consideration or thoughtfulness.

Recent events have highlighted how little progress football has made under the Football Association campaign of similar title.

I choose to say football rather than the FA, because all too often people in football, especially the upper echelon, eschew responsibility in the same way that people blame society for their predicament rather than themselves.

Consider the David Norris matter. The Ipswich player caused outrage by making a 'handcuffs' gesture, supporting a former team-mate who has robbed the Peak family of Arron (ten) and Ben (eight) by dangerous driving while drunk.

The club's statement read: 'David deeply regrets that his actions have been wrongly interpreted and has written a personal and private letter of regret to Mr and Mrs Peak. In hearing the player's explanation, the club also regrets the potential for misinterpretation of the gesture and would love to make a donation to an appropriate charity, equal to the fine imposed on the player.'

This insult dressed up as an apology is reprehensible and has the hallmark of being drafted by a smart-arse lawyer. Norris is said here not to regret his action, only the allegedly wrong interpretation thereof; Ipswich only regret the possibility of such inaccurate deduction; nor do they have the guts to tell us what the action meant.

The reason we are not enlightened is because the explanation, whenever it was dreamt up, is so fanciful it would not be believed. If it was that simple they would have immediately told us, so we would realise we had done the poor lad a mischief.

Further, the reference to charity can be seen as a deeply cynical way of trying to show that they are a caring club. It says everything that through monetary payment they think they will be absolved.

The Professional Footballers' Association are said to have condemned the actions – why, if it was an innocent gesture misinterpreted? Their ever-present apologist Gordon Taylor said it was probably done in ignorance rather than maliciously.

The PFA chief executive said: 'It's totally inappropriate and I'm extremely sorry that he did that. I am sure he is sorry too and my apologies would go to the family of Mrs Peak who lost two sons. In fairness to the lad, he could not have realised the consequence of his actions.'

It says much about the way Taylor is prepared to spin for his members, even in the face of such distaste. How does he know it was ignorant and not malicious?

Why could Norris not see the consequences; because he is too thick, or because they were impossible to see? Neither position is acceptable.

Why is Taylor apologising to the family? He was not involved; moreover, if there is, as claimed, an alternative explanation, it is needless.

Carl Day, acting chair of the Ipswich Town Supporters Trust, said Norris's actions could never be condoned, but that the club's punishment was apt, and banning the player would serve no purpose. 'They haven't sat back and taken it lightly. If the player was banned he would still be paid, although the team would be weakened.'

There we have it – the real focus from all these statements: the club's welfare comes first.

Respect? It makes me want to vomit.

The campaign resulted from a detailed survey of all levels of football which identified the abuse and lack of respect within football as the number one concern. Though the professional game disagrees, there is a genuine level of disgust within football at the example they and their players set every week.

Some seven thousand officials drop out of the game every year due to the treatment they receive from players, spectators and fans. If that doesn't concern all in football, they deserve what they get.

While I agree the solving of this should be a priority, I vehemently disagree with the way the FA have approached the issue.

Take a look at the video supporting the campaign on the Football Association website. It shows a former professional and amateur players turning up to find there is no referee. They play without one, leading to innocent and playful shenanigans and decide that a referee is essential, but nobody will do it; even the £6 million man, Mr Capello.

This video should have included the numerous examples of the vile abuse, assault and confrontation suffered by referees at all levels.

The reality would then be plain and when, no, if, the FA decides to use whatever necessary measures to stop it, nobody could claim they were disproportionate.

All they need to do is one of two things. Warn every player, club and manager that next weekend referees will give a yellow card for every example of dissent. If a player gets two yellows for such acts, off he goes; the same for managers, but they go to the stand.

Then, and this is the crucial point, when the managers, chairmen and fans whine, say, 'Tough. This is the way it's going to be. Get in line, or get out.' Also, for every ten cards picked up for this conduct, a club is deducted three points.

Alternatively, mark the middle of the goal line. Whenever dissent occurs, the referee marches ten yards towards that mark, centralising the resultant place of the free-kick. Then, and this is also crucial, if his ten-yard advance takes him into the penalty area, he awards a penalty.

The most effective behaviour modifiers are peer-group pressure and self-interest. Once points are lost through penalties or card accumulation, managers, team-mates and fans will ensure dissent stops. At present, managers do not deal with this as it costs them nothing. See how quickly they act when vital points are lost and their employment threatened.

Unfair? No, this behaviour is not accepted in any other sport; that such simple measures will be called ridiculous or draconian simply shows how abnormal is football's acceptance of abuse.

It would be over in two months. There might be months of carnage, bleating, wailing and gnashing of teeth, but wouldn't that be a small price to pay?

In the end it comes down to this – does the FA want to sort it out or not?

20

England's 2003 World Cup hero Jonny Wilkinson is now obsessed with relaxing

November 2008

The defined medical term for an extreme reaction or form of behaviour which is outside the norm is pathological. This has all sorts of unhelpful connotations, but in its clinical sense it perfectly describes the behaviour displayed by both the 'old' and 'new' Jonny Wilkinson.

Once the stuff of legend, Wilkinson's description of his obsessive training, especially kicking, always seemed to me to border on the extreme.

Following his analysis of his performances throughout his unfortunate, yet stellar, career I recognised the unmistakable traits of obsession, for I share many of them. Rarely did you hear Wilkinson dwell on the things he had done brilliantly; much more likely was a rueful smile/grimace over the few decisions he got wrong, or the mistakes he felt he had made.

This self-criticism is invaluable as a tool to spur a player to even greater effort; many players are incapable of honesty when it comes to scrutinising their performances, seeking to apportion blame elsewhere: a team-mate, bad luck, or most likely the referee if you are a footballer.

However, when it becomes excessive, it becomes a hindrance in sport; as a tenet by which to live your life it is a disaster. In search of perfection on the field you seek the same in everyday matters and as it is impossible not to make mistakes, the vicious criticism that helps in sport is the source of constant dissatisfaction. In short, you become a miserable bastard.

Furthermore, as Wilkinson admits, this approach to sport leads to such single-minded focus that you lose sight of nearly every-thing else; thus, when a game goes well you are high, but obviously taking into account the multiple errors you convince yourself you committed; when it goes badly, the sky darkens and you just brood.

The long periods of rehabilitation cannot have helped Wilkinson; whatever he says, there must have been times when he despaired and raged at the sheer unfairness of it all. Towards the end of his latest stint with England, many commentators said he needed to relax more; without knowing why he now faced such a conundrum, they were nevertheless correct. Eventually obsession affects everything you try to do and it was affecting Wilkinson, who was simply trying too hard and forcing plays which he needed to recognise were not the right option.

It seems that his transformation has come through reading extensively about Buddhism. Unlike some, I do not ridicule this bout of self-awareness and all who do are fools. However, the description given by Wilkinson about his introduction and devel-opment of some of its teaching is interesting. He says he read massively into things – again total dedication to the learning cause. I will go for months not reading a novel; then I will read fifteen back-to-back, often long into the night. His pursuance of knowl-edge betrays obsession.

He sounds happier in himself and that is good, but I listened carefully to a long interview he did with Brian Alexander on Radio 5 Live on Thursday night. The overwhelming impression he left was again one of obsession. He sounded so relaxed, so in tune with himself, that it came across as slightly surreal; as if he was now trying with all his might to be the happiest, most sorted person in the world.

Whether he accepts or recognises this, the volte-face is so extreme that I fear it is unsustainable. Being in a state of contentment is good, but again it cannot be real all the time. There are things that should anger him, should make him want to stand up and shout, fight, become belligerent. This is also part of sport and life.

Wilkinson at some point will face the spectre of retirement, which is a subject few players know how to approach. His present philosophy will help and he will need it because the total change is very difficult. For a person of the psyche of Wilkinson it will be even more challenging. There is not the space to dive into the topic, though it would be interesting in itself; suffice to say it seems that even a sportswoman of the brilliance of Martina Navratilova has found the loss of public adulation sufficiently difficult to compel her to appear on *I'm a Celebrity . . . Get Me Out of Here!* She mixes with well-known people, but not necessarily celebrities, and may, in a quiet, later, moment wonder what motivated her.

The perfect existence is not something allowed to most of us, but it is to be found somewhere between Wilkinson's two incarnations; certainly nearer to the present, but the two facets must coexist for they are both ineffably part of him.

Until he relaxes about being relaxed he will find the present incarnation no more a solution than the first – though at least he won't be a miserable bastard!

21

The Rain Tax

Introduction

The private utility companies, created by the Conservatives, are effectively monopoly suppliers. Where gas and electricity are supplied there is a notional ability to switch providers but it is very limited; when it comes to water there is no choice at all. With a lot of effort you could live without gas or electricity but not water; it is this fact that makes the role of the two consumer bodies that are meant to protect our interests so important. This is a tale of woeful inadequacy, if not downright nefariousness by Ofwat and the Consumer Council for Water.

Charges for the use of drains for sewerage and rain water are a standard item and used to be assessed, as far as non-domestic consumers were concerned, on the ratable value of the consumer's property. This meant that charities, churches, sports clubs and other socially useful organizations gained rebates from this charge.

In 2007 Ofwat, despite there being no complaints about the system, took it upon themselves to recommend to the water utilities that they change the basis for this charge. They did this because they looked at one line of the guideline legislation that said Ofwat had to ensure 'there was no undue discrimination between non-domestic customers'. They argued that ratable value charging breached this principle because, for example, a small shop in a town centre with a higher ratable value was charged more than a much bigger store out of town where the rates were lower. This was effectively a cross-subsidy and had to be stopped.

The new system was one which charged consumers according to the surface area of their property. The reasoning was that a larger property caught more rain, this went into the drains and this way each consumer would be charged for the strain it placed on the system. The anomalies created by this flawed reasoning soon became apparent but it was not until United Utilities Plc. levied its extraordinary increased bills that opposition was galvanised.

As you will see, despite everybody, including eventually the relevant Government department DEFRA, telling Ofwat and the CWW, which supported Ofwat at every turn, they were wrong, Ofwat remained intransigent to the last, refusing to alter their stance at all until forced to do so by legislation.

This is how your regulatory bodies work for you today and unless you happen to have a newspaper column, there is not a lot you can do about it.

Don't let our local sports clubs go down the drain because of water charges

January 2009

Here's a tip for those investors wanting to make rich pickings: a newspaper recently predicted '[for] straightforward value-for-money, look no further than the utilities, which were remarkable in 2008 for the level of price rises they managed to push through. United Utilities yields almost seven per cent.'

That United Utilities Plc (UUP), which provides some seven million customers in the North West of England with water, is seen by tipsters as an excellent bet is hardly surprising. Along with its fellow utility companies it is a virtual monopoly; able to impose its charges and ensure handsome dividends. Its profits for the years 2005 to 2007 inclusive totalled £974,800,000.

In 2007, its shareholders pocketed £1,500,000,000, following the sale of UUP's electricity interests (in the same year UUP made a thousand workers redundant, saving £400,000,000). Added to that, UUP's household customers have been told their bills will rise by 2.7 per cent above inflation every year across the 2010 to 2015 period.

Yet, not content with bleeding its domestic customers, UUP's actions now threaten to cause the extinction of many small volunteer sports clubs in the North West – ones run solely for the benefit of their members, which rely on the goodwill of tens of thousands of people, some of whom devote thousands of hours a year to running their clubs: tennis, cricket, bowling and others. The concern is that others may also be doing the same.

The reason? In 2007, UUP – whose website highlights its work in education and the community – changed the way it charges non-domestic users for surface and highway drainage, using the surface area of their property ('site-area charging'), rather than their council tax banding as the basis. This has caused astonishing increases in previous bills. The following examples are taken from a huge number of letters I have received from clubs:

Mellor Sports Club, Stockport: present charge £800 p.a., rising to £6,000 in 2010

Sphynx Tennis Club, Southport: £860 p.a., rising to £2,580 in 2010

Clitheroe Cricket, Bowling and Tennis Club: £200 p.a., rising to £3,000 in 2011

Ashton-under-Lyne Cricket and Bowling Club: £1,000 p.a., rising to £2,002 next year [2010].

Many of those writing to me express real fears that their club will fold if UUP is allowed to continue making such increases. Unsurprising: the percentage increases above range from 100 to 1,400 per cent. But UUP claims that it can only rate customers as domestic or non-domestic; as such, community clubs are bracketed with small and multinational companies – such as the pharmaceutical giant ICI in Warrington.

Mike Tyldesley, the honorary secretary of the Little Hulton Cricket and Bowling Club in Manchester, says his club's experience is common: 'Our charges will increase from approximately £280 for waste water to approximately £1,100 over the next three years,' he says, 'for a very small area of car park, mostly shale, which soaks away naturally.'

To make matters worse, the way UUP has applied these changes has been shambolic. Clubs claim they have been charged for areas they do not own; there have been threats to cut off those that do not pay and months of inactivity on the complaints. As

Tyldesley says, 'We have been paying United Utilities the old rate for waste water, but they have now tried to cut off our supply.'

Yet Ofwat, the water regulator, appears unwilling to stop these huge increases and, as such, UUP claims it is doing nothing untoward. However, Ofwat's guidelines to water companies state, 'Companies who are thinking of introducing site-area charging need to assess possible impacts on all customers' bills. In particular, companies will need to take into account the scale and speed of any bill changes to see if they are reasonable and acceptable to customers . . . We request that companies demonstrate that their current household and non-household charges are cost-reflective.'

For drainage for an impermeable area – such as a car park – measuring up to 11,999 square metres, UUP charges £10,896. Yet Yorkshire Water charges £298.72 for the same area, and some water utility companies have decided not to charge in this way at all. (Only four of the ten companies that deal with waste water nationwide – Severn Trent, Yorkshire Water, Northumbrian Water and UUP – have chosen to switch to this method of charging.)

So how can UUP claim their charges are cost-reflective when on the other side of the Pennines the same service appears to be provided at a fraction of the cost, and in other areas there are no similar charges? Ofwat's answer is that UUP will not profit as a result of these charges. But this is of no consequence when considering the effects of the changes.

These community clubs are recognised by their local councils, the Inland Revenue and HM Customs & Excise as being non-profit organisations, thus different from businesses; they receive up to an 80 per cent rebate on their council charges. UUP is unwilling to so differentiate.

I realise the principle of non-profit is unfamiliar to UUP, so let me explain it – and the clubs to which it applies. Around the country, a huge number of small clubs have been founded and are run by volunteers. The sums of money involved are generally relatively small, certainly compared to UUP's profit and dividends; this means significant increases in costs are disproportionately destructive.

Since no profit is sought or made, the clubs keep membership fees as low as possible, allowing hundreds of thousands of ordinary people of all ages, both sexes and all races to exercise and socialise – with all the concomitant benefits for those individuals and wider society.

The village or town club has been and is an expression of something becoming all too rare in England: individuals taking responsibility for their own affairs; organising and running things without waiting for the Government or council to provide. It is indisputable that they provide near-essential facilities for members, without draining local taxpayers.

Many ageing club members rely on clubs for their social interaction. In deprived areas, such places provide an alternative to the more destructive activities pursued by many youths. And in areas with large ethnic communities, clubs, especially cricket clubs, allow racial interaction in a friendly and challenging environment.

Do I really need to go on?

You would think that the threat of closure of these clubs would be an important matter to the Government. Not so. In a column for this newspaper's Sport section last month I challenged individual ministers to back my call for either a change in the categorisation of non-profit community clubs exempting them from the increased charges, or that they are given a rebate by UUP.

The response? Nothing, zilch, *nada*.

This could, of course, be the result of normal Government incompetence. It could be the normal fear of upsetting any big business or the normal over-reliance on Government-created and ineffective regulatory bodies. Whatever the reason, it is not good enough.

So, I repeat these calls, armed with the certainty that I speak for a very significant number of clubs and individuals. Andy

Burnham, as Secretary of State for Culture, Media and Sport, are you going to allow these clubs to fold because of the actions of UUP?

Hazel Blears, as Secretary of State for Communities and Local Government, I have listed the contributions these clubs make. Is sport only part of your community when there is a convenient photo-opportunity?

Ed Miliband, as the relevant Secretary of State for Energy and Climate change, sort this out. All it needs is the will – have you got it?

I care not whether UUP, Ofwat or the Government resolve this, but I, and thousands of people who have not the wherewithal to fight, want it resolving before irreparable damage is done.

Many investors now look at the business of a company, as well as its share price and yield, before they buy. Whatever the rewards, is it right to support a company that is effectively in the process of dismantling our sporting heritage? Are you happy to be complicit in this?

A spokesman for UUP said the charging method was recommended by Ofwat and approved by the Consumer Council for Water, saying, 'We are just the water provider; Ofwat is the regulator. If that's their preferred method of charging, then that's the method that we will use . . .

'We are not able to distinguish between a charity, or a sports club and a business when it comes to charging . . . We gave a detailed map of the area to be charged for and we asked customers to come back and ask if that area was right.

'Some did, some didn't. If they still think the area is wrong, they should give us a call and we will without doubt come out and have a look at it.'

A spokesman for Ofwat said, 'We think charging by site area is the fairest because it is cost-reflective.' But he said Ofwat had no legal powers to insist that companies are charged on the new basis.

Petition update: save our sports clubs from water bill disaster

January 2009

My campaign for a better deal for small sports clubs has attracted widespread support, but much more is needed. I have been backed by the ECB and RFU, but the FA has not responded.

Having written to every Labour MP in the North West, only three responded: Claire Curtis-Thomas, Brian Iddon and Peter Kilfoyle; but all were supportive, with Iddon stating he is trying to raise a question in the House on 12 January. Further, I understand that Andy Burnham visited two cricket clubs two days ago in Iddon's constituency – he is thus fully aware of this issue.

If your MP is not one of those specified, please write, e-mail, or call them and ask why they are not assisting.

None of the Government ministers mentioned in the previous article – Burnham, Blears and Miliband – has bothered to respond. To make it worse, I am aware from a reader's letter that Burnham has known about this problem since at least 31 March 2008. Neither have their Tory counterparts (Pickles, Hunt and Clark) responded, despite each having been contacted by me.

Outstanding answers are awaited to detailed inquiries I made of Ofwat, but at least they replied, unlike the MPs. From United Utilities – well, what do you think?

Comments on the petition make it clear that there is real anger and fear over the activities of UUP. The contributions below are representative of the tenor of responses and because of these I will not give up this fight until this iniquitous situation is resolved.

Water charge protest making progress

January 2009

I want a fairer category for community sports clubs exempting them, or giving rebates, from recently changed and substantially increased bills for drainage. Your support for this campaign is working. Gerry Sutcliffe, the Minister for Sport, tells me he is talking to Ofwat, the Water Services Regulation Authority. Jeremy Hunt, the shadow culture secretary, has signed the petition.

Ofwat now state: 'The policy is right, but the roll-out by United Utilities [UUP, the UK's largest listed water company] was wrong. The company failed to appreciate the impact these changes would have on certain types of customers.

'We believe they mishandled communications with customers. Customers were left confused about both the fairness and environmental benefits of charging by site area. We are pleased our discussions with United Utilities have resulted in the company freezing the charge at 2008/09 levels for affected faith buildings, community amateur sports clubs, as well as Guide and Scout Association properties.

'This action gives customers breathing space, and UUP time to implement the policy in a clear way. No customer is out of pocket.

'This charge means organizations will need to take responsibility for the drainage of their properties. This will help reduce the likelihood of flooding – an issue that cannot be ignored, as the 2007 floods in Yorkshire and Humberside showed.

'Customers broadly pay for the service they receive, whereas in the previous system some customers subsidised others. You had an unfair situation where a small city centre newsagent could in effect end up paying in part for services used by a large out-of-town factory.'

Ofwat maintain that the alteration is the Government's responsibility. But Huw Irranca-Davies, Parliamentary Under-Secretary at the Department for Environment, Food and Rural Affairs (DEFRA), says Ofwat are responsible for charging policies. Further, 'Those making similar demands on services should be charged on the same basis', but they (DEFRA) were 'actively considering what may be done' and 'undertaking to review how the charges are rolled out.'

On the above, I say:

a) This is a cynical attempt to stem bad publicity, sideline the issue by claiming the initiative must be given a chance, then carry on as before.

b) It gives MPs every excuse to disengage. A year from now they might claim a resolution impractical due to General Election demands.

c) UUP did not fail to appreciate the impact of their practice. They did not care.

d) Clubs are not confused. They complain these charges are unfair.

e) Why should clubs be grateful? This is akin to a mugger saying it is partly your fault.

f) UUP can maintain the same increased charges post-moratorium.

g) The 2007 report referred to concrete or asphalt surfaces exacerbating flooding. Cricket, rugby and bowls do not use such.

h) The change does not ensure similar demands on services are charged on the same basis – an office the size of a sports field has either plants or people using water. This and all rainfall on its roof runs into the drains. A sports field absorbs all water.

i) This 'fairer' system now sees small volunteer clubs paying in part for services used by large businesses.

j) Sporting clubs are a unique case.

k) While similarly meritorious, sport's case is based on the impossibility of alternatives. It cannot be played in a clubhouse and clubs cannot minimise their surface area without ceasing to function.

l) Yorkshire Water charge under £300 for draining an area for which UUP charge almost £12,000 (approximately 4,000 per cent more) – how is this disparity justifiable?

I suggest Gerry Sutcliffe visits Hilary Benn, Secretary of State at DEFRA, and explains that the principle and application of these changed bills require rectification. If just one club consequently folds in twelve months' time, they will not be forgiven.

Finally, an apology for wrongly stating last week (15 January) that Tom Drury is a director of UUP. Tom left the board in March 2007 and is not responsible for UUP's current business practices.

Ofwat–*Daily Telegraph* e-mails

February 2009

This exchange of e-mails typified Ofwat's approach to my campaign. I am told it was a similar story in respect of all the other groups that had to deal with this organisation.

> Sent: 5 February 2009
> From: Tony Moran [mailto:Tony.Moran@ofwat.gsi.gov.uk]
> To: William Lewis (*Daily Telegraph*) [WL was the editor-in-chief at the time]
> Cc: Brian Moore
> Subject: Brian Moore column – inappropriate use of Ofwat e-mail address
>
> Dear Mr Lewis,
> I am writing to express our concern and deep dismay at the inclusion of an entirely inappropriate e-mail address in Brian Moore's column in today's *Daily Telegraph* ('Rain tax protest taken to the heart of Government – we will not go away', Thursday 5 February 2009).
> Mr Moore asked readers who supported his petition to e-mail Defra, Consumer Council for Water and Ofwat to register their support for his campaign against changes to the way some water and sewerage companies charge for surface water drainage.

In a piece of sloppy, lazy and unprofessional journalism, Mr Moore saw fit to include an e-mail address for our press office team. This is a clear abuse of a dedicated facility set up to assist journalists requiring information and assistance from our media team. It is intended for the sole purpose of making possible a dialogue between Ofwat and the media.

We are happy to provide an appropriate e-mail address for your readers to contact us on the issue of surface water drainage and charging by site area. We trust that you will ensure Mr Moore does not abuse his position as a journalist by publishing the press office e-mail address again.

Yours sincerely,

Tony Moran, Head of Communications, Ofwat

6 February 2009

From: David Bond (*Daily Telegraph*, Sports Editor)

To: Tony Moran, Ofwat

Re: 'Rain Tax' protest taken to heart of government – we will not go away

Dear Mr Moran

Further to your e-mail exchange with our consulting editor yesterday, I write to confirm that the change from pressofficeteam@ to enquiries@ofwat.gsi.gov.uk has been effected and is now live online: http://www.telegraph.co.uk/sport/4515278/Rain-Tax-protest-taken-to-heart-of-Government.html

While we have been prepared to accede to your request, I must make clear that the *Daily Telegraph* rejects your criticism of Brian Moore. Mr Moore's writings about the surface water drainage charges have addressed issues of considerable public interest and concern. His petition has attracted tremendous support and, as he makes clear in his latest piece, the campaign will continue unabated.

It was entirely appropriate for Mr Moore to exhort our readers to back the petition by recording their support directly with Ofwat as well as with the Department for Environment, Food and Rural Affairs. Further, it was perfectly reasonable for him to suppose that the communication of such public backing would be more immediate and effective if addressed to Ofwat's communications department, i.e. using your department's e-mail address.

The 'Contacting us' section of Ofwat's website does not in fact specify any e-mail address for the communication of grievances about the policy and level of charges regarding surface water drainage. Regarding 'complaints from customers about their water company' the complainant is merely told to contact the Consumer Council for Water. The only e-mail address given, namely, enquiries@ofwat.gsi.gov.uk, is said to be for those who 'would like' Ofwat to contact them.

In the circumstances, instead of impugning Mr Moore's professional skills and integrity without justification and in defamatory terms as you have done, perhaps you may care to conduct a reappraisal of your organisation's website and provide a dedicated e-mail address for use by those wishing to lodge protests of this kind.

Yours sincerely

David Bond

Sports Editor

'Rain Tax' moratorium won't register for some

February 2009

The moratorium on imposing the 'rain tax' – the increase in drainage charges levied by water companies that threaten the existence of sports clubs – announced recently by Ofwat and United Utilities Plc was publicly declared to be for all 'the affected faith buildings, sports clubs and community centres'.

I am now told by one club that UUP are still to charge clubs not registered as Community Amateur Sports Clubs. Registration is not mandatory; for some it is disadvantageous, as it adds expense and administrative burden. Nevertheless, those not registered provide the same community and wider benefits and any such discrimination against them would be a further act of perniciousness by UUP.

Ofwat told me I should make urgent inquiries of UUP, as they are administering the moratorium. Ofwat chose the words that outlined the deal. Thus, they are responsible if volunteers and ordinary sports people have been misled. Instead of trying to, yet again, pass the buck, Ofwat should get off their backside and start doing their job, which is regulating the water industry and looking after consumers.

The deafening silence on water charges speaks volumes

April 2009

To date, the campaign to prevent Ofwat (the Water Services Regulation Commission) imposing a changed system of charging for drainage in respect of community sports clubs and other volunteer organisations has achieved a moratorium from United Utilities Plc. However, the silence from DEFRA and Ofwat concerning the future of these charges says much about the way Government and supposedly consumer-friendly quangos operate.

I predicted that this freeze was merely an attempt to kick the issue into the long grass and then carry on as before and I was right. From those responsible, no change; no permanent exemption and continued weasel words and passing of the buck.

I sent Ofwat a detailed list of questions and received direct answers to only some, and the use of sophistry in other answers that would have made George Orwell blush.

Ofwat maintains it is bound by a guiding clause in the relevant legislation that states there must be no undue discrimination in charging between non-domestic consumers. As a former law partner, I am aware that drafters of contracts and statutes never use an ambiguous word like 'undue' unless they mean it to confer an element of discretion; the reason plainly being that any ambiguity allows subjective interpretation. If they had meant no discrimination, which is what Ofwat is effectively saying, they would not have added the word 'undue', as it is unnecessary; worse, it is positively dangerous.

The highlighted words are a double negative and, properly read, mean that there can be due discrimination, which is what we are asking for. I asked Ofwat very detailed questions about this and asked it to explain its interpretation of this wording. They would not answer in kind.

What we have here is a body, which is supposed to represent the little man, not only interpreting a crucial guideline wrongly, but choosing to interpret it against the interests of the very bodies that most need its protection.

Ofwat says that UUP's moratorium does not break its interpretation because there is no element of cross-subsidy (i.e. the costs involved being absorbed by the utility and not non-domestic concumers); UUP taking up the shortfall of the temporarily reduced charges from its considerable profits.

In short, Ofwat will not change its anti-sports club stance, continuing to claim DEFRA must enact legislation if it is to alter its erroneous stance. From DEFRA there has also been no further action.

It is now becoming clear that today you have to make as much trouble as possible before those that should listen do listen. The next in a number of actions planned is the UUP shareholders meeting in the summer. I urge all of you to buy a UUP share and, as is your right, raise this at the AGM, asking for UUP to grant permanent exemptions from increases on drainage charges to community sports clubs and similar organisations.

You must also continue to e-mail Ofwat and DEFRA about this. I realise that sustaining the enthusiasm for continued campaigning is difficult, but that is just what these bodies want; don't let them get away with it. Keep shouting, keep protesting.

Rain tax update: time for us to take action to end water companies' iniquitous rain tax

July 2009

Recent changes to the way water companies charge consumers for surface water drainage has led to crippling increases in bills for the least well-off. Increases of up to 3,000 per cent have been claimed, but who is the villain of the rain tax scandal? It is Ofwat, whose self-proclaimed duties include protecting the interests of consumers, including vulnerable groups.

On 9 February 2007 Ofwat stated that before implementing a new policy proposal it was for the water companies to carry out this task, even though this appears to conflict with paragraph 39 of the memorandum.

A similar attempt to shift responsibility was exposed when Ofwat gave partial answers to questions I raised about this affair. Despite having flexibility within existing legislation to allow due discrimination between consumers, Ofwat is interpreting its power expressly against vulnerable voluntary bodies. They claim it is for Government to act to allow exemption from charges.

Ofwat this week refused to alter its anti-volunteer stance and effectively ignored protests from Scout groups. It prefers to listen to big business and adopts their language as it insists that everybody must pay the same amount, irrespective of their income.

Such regressive taxation has long been abandoned as unfair, but they are happy for it to apply to the rain tax.

Its frequent use of the word 'stakeholder' is the sort of management-speak rubbish that is used to confuse people. These are real people who, on a daily basis, make a difference, thousands of ordinary men and women who give up their time to organise sport and provide the benefits for all.

Although those of us who care about the survival of small volunteer groups are receiving increasing support from MPs, it is astounding that the House of Commons snubbed the protests by refusing entry to the Scouts, saying that because they could not vote they could not lobby.

A spokesman for the Commons authorities said he wanted to 'establish the full facts' before commenting. How many more facts does he need? The boys concerned understand the problem, yet their opinions do not count; and they wonder why there is widespread youth apathy with the political process.

On 15 July you have the chance to make your feelings known to these people by attending the campaign meeting from 2 p.m. in the House of Commons. It is a public meeting and unless you are a Scout they cannot throw you out.

The importance of the meeting is highlighted by the fact that Philip Fletcher, the Chair of Ofwat's Board, will be attending to represent the regulator. Huw Irranca-Davies, from DEFRA, will also attend in addition to forty-five other MPs. Come and help secure a vital change to this iniquitous tax.

Rain tax: victory in *Telegraph* campaign to save sports clubs

October 2009

Those of you who signed the *Telegraph* Sport petition, demanding a rebate from the rain tax for community-based, non-profit sports clubs, churches and other volunteer organisations, have helped persuade the Government to legislate to force Ofwat to introduce a social tariff, which will mean lower bills.

When United Utilities Plc, following Ofwat's recommendation, altered the way it charged for surface water drainage by charging per square metre and not rateable value, increases in bills of up to 2,000 per cent resulted.

Complainants got nowhere because DEFRA, the relevant Government department, claimed it could not interfere with the regulator. Ofwat maintained it was a good idea and was supported by the Consumer Council for Water. United Utilities said it was only following orders.

Individual clubs were threatened with having their water cut off if they didn't pay and when they appealed had to provide professional drawings in support.

Ofwat condoned United Utilities claiming money without having to prove its bills were accurate, completely the opposite to normal business where a supplier has to justify a bill.

Severn Trent, which voluntarily discounted clubs' bills, was told by Ofwat to abandon its socially aware policy. In the face of an intransigent monopoly supplier and no help from quangos established to protect the consumer, many clubs paid up.

Since early 2008, the Church tried to work within the system to persuade MPs to pressure Ofwat to revise its stance, but to no avail. Before *Telegraph* Sport's campaign, the Rugby Football Union and Lawn Tennis Association had complained, and Mike Gatting, on behalf of the England and Wales Cricket Board, had spent six fruitless months trying to get someone to listen.

My experience is that by all means try polite debate, but when it does not work you have to agitate. The main difficulty in fighting the rain tax was that individually a small sports club had no clout; combining clubs across many sports and involving their national governing bodies not only gave a focal point for protest, it gave credibility.

The RFU, ECB and LTA offered their full support immediately. The one sport conspicuous by its absence of support was football. My attempts to contact Brian Mawhinney, the Football League chairman, went unanswered; numerous calls to the Football Association and three voice messages and three texts to Adrian Bevington, the FA director of communications, were completely ignored. Not until recently did the FA lend its name to our campaign and then only when it seemed likely to be successful. In contrast, ordinary football supporters urged their own clubs to sign our petition through fan sites like those of both Manchester City and United.

In the end, MPs' support is crucial, because only they have the power to force change through legislation; but merely talking to politicians only gets you so far. As MPs face demands from similar causes, only by getting enough people to complain through letters, e-mails and in MPs' surgeries did we make this issue actionable.

The first e-mail I sent to all forty-five Labour MPs in the North West received only a handful of responses. When I followed up with a more forthright e-mail, referring to this column, the replies tripled.

Public criticism is a potent weapon and asking questions of Andy Burnham, the then Minister for Sport, made him address the issue with colleagues at DEFRA like Hilary Benn and Huw Irranca-Davies. Early Day Motions were laid down by Peter Kilfoyle and things began to move.

Unfortunately, the media has a short attention span, so we had to find ways of keeping the story fresh. When Gatting and I went to hand in the petition to DEFRA, the potential for unfavourable coverage in the news got us a two-hour meeting during which Mike put the case in a considered way and I shouted a lot, highlighting the blunders made by Ofwat in misreading statutory guidelines and misinterpreting the proper meaning of clauses in legislation. In combination we left the minister in no doubt that we would not let this issue go away.

Ofwat is supposed to represent our interests in an industry with monopoly suppliers; not so with water. Given our unique vulnerability Ofwat should be a Rottweiler regulator, but it is a poodle; the more criticism Ofwat received, the greater became its determination not to be seen to U-turn.

In May this year I attended the General Synod debate at which Philip Fletcher, Ofwat's chairman, gave an utterly ineffectual defence of the regulator's position.

Despite everyone else telling Ofwat it was wrong, the best it could do was broker a cessation of United Utilities bills for a year, during which it explained that United Utilities would tell its confused consumers why the new charges were a good thing environmentally, then it would be allowed to bill at the same rate – big deal.

Due to the resilience of the campaigners a seminal meeting of the Commons All-Party Scout Group was held at Portcullis House, Westminster, on 20 July 2009. In attendance were a large number of MPs and, crucially, Irranca-Davies and Fletcher.

Having been in the Boys' Brigade I thought it kind that I was allowed to address the group and a packed public gallery, and, having gone through the various intellectual arguments, I ended by telling the MPs that if Ofwat would not do its job, the MPs should do theirs and sort this out as the little people were tired of buck-passing and didn't care how the result was achieved.

DEFRA's recent announcement shows that your support and that of thousands of other ordinary people has finally worked. That it will take legislation to force Ofwat to do the decent thing is a disgrace and Fletcher and chief executive Regina Finn, as the top Ofwat executives, should go.

However, we then run into the wider point – how are quangos regulated? As they cost the taxpayer between £34 billion and £60 billion per annum and sixty-eight quango bosses earn more than £194,000, the route of responsibility should be clear and we should know how to sack those responsible for things like the rain tax.

Reader Comments

Here are just a few of thousands of comments of support from the petition. They highlight not only the anger and dismay at the inaction of Government and the appointed regulators, but also show that Ofwat's claim that people did not understand the issues was palpably untrue:

'The comment "We are just the water provider . . . we are not able to distinguish between a business or sports club and a charity . . ." shows just what contempt these businesses have for the intelligence of the general public. It's high time we refused to accept any old answer and stopped the erosion of our local sports facilities and amenities.' John Shaw

'I fully back your petition. I have written to UUP and Ofwat, on behalf of Romiley Cricket Club and they were completely unsympathetic and hide behind legislation. The rates for the cricket club will go up from £178 to over £1,200 by 2010. This is of course in addition to the metered water charge which is in the region of £600.

'As you pointed out, they do not appear to understand what non-profit making organisations are. I also contacted Andy Burnham who did not even bother to reply, and the shadow minister for sport who did but was unaware of the situation but said he would pursue the matter.

'All a complete waste of time. Nevertheless, good luck with your petition.' Maurice Stafford

'I fully support this campaign. I am the treasurer of Norley Hall Cricket Club and although we are registered as a charity by our local authority we have been forced to pay the drainage charges – after a two-year battle with United Utilities the threat to turn off our water forced us to pay.' Graham Dean

'As President of the Amateur Football Alliance with more than four hundred clubs, all run by volunteers, I think that I can speak for all of them in supporting this campaign. Well done, Brian, in raising awareness.' Malcolm Perks

I set out here a list of clubs that supported the petition, firstly to show how widespread the effect of this situation was, and secondly to show that most of the clubs listed are of the archetypal volunteer community variety that do so much good for us all.

Supporting clubs:

Southport and District Tennis League

Staffordshire Rugby Union

Bolton RUFC

Stanwix Bowling Club, Carlisle

Havering Cricket Club

Kingsley CC

Belvedere & Caldervale Sports Club

New Brighton Rugby Club, Lancashire

Crown Green Bowls Club, Settle, North Yorkshire

Clitheroe Cricket, Bowling and Tennis Club

Manchester Rugby and Cheadle Hulme Cricket Club

Chorley Cricket Club

Pontefract RUFC

Mellor Sports Club

Royston Cricket Club

Lostock Gralam FC

Ulverston Cricket Club

Wigan Cricket Development Group

Chard Town AFC

Workington Cricket Club

Tintwistle Cricket Club, Derbyshire

Shenfield Cricket Club, Hertfordshire

Rugby Club, Tarleton

Barnby Dun Cricket Club, Doncaster

Accrington West Scout Group

Chatsworth Tennis Club, Carlisle

Luctonians Sports Club, Kingsland

Warton Cricket Club (Nr Carnforth, Lancs)

Vernon-Carus Sports Club

Wigton Cricket Club

Lancashire County RFU

Botany Bay Cricket Club

Langleybury Cricket Club, Hertfordshire

Avon RFC

Ashford Hockey Club, Kent

Tyldesley RUFC

Cheadle Heath Sports Club

President of Rochdale RUFC

Heywood Cricket Club

Penrith Rugby Club

Penrith Friars Bowling Club

Pendle RUFC

Didsbury Toc H RUFC

Rochdale RUFC

Wigan RFC

Warton Cricket Club

Newbury RFC

Sussex Cricket

Freshfield Bowling Club, Timms Lane,
   Formby

Bristol Greenbank Bowling Club

Hoylake RFC

Odiham & N. Warnborough Bowling
   Club, Hampshire

Littlemore Rugby Club

Clay Lane Sports Club

Anselmians RFC

Peterborough RUFC

Ashton-on-Mersey RUFC

Marple RUFC

Birkenhead Park Football Club

Falkland Cricket Club

Enfield Cricket Club

Barnton Cricket Club in Cheshire

Elvaston Cricket Club

Mottram Cricket Club

Garstang Rugby Club

Bognor RFC

Stafford RUFC

Horden RFC

Droylsden Youth Centre

Ryecroft Park Sports Club

Duffield Squash and Tennis Clubs

Cannock Cricket & Hockey Club

22

Mocking Michael Phelps's achievements is truly pathetic

January 2009

I had a couple of half-smiles during *Most Annoying People* of 2008 on BBC3. Sniggering at Piers Morgan is not very difficult, nor very inventive, but criticism of Michael Phelps, the winner of eight gold medals in the pool in Beijing, demonstrated a few British traits I hate. A string of 'comedians', so famous and successful that their names were continually flashed up to tell us who they were, let rip.

Phelps was decried as annoying because he was just too good. I may be thick and have missed the comic device, but have we become such a nation of losers that outstanding achievement is risible in itself?

If not annoying for his success, Phelps was boring. Nick Faldo, Nigel Mansell, Jonny Wilkinson – the list of sporting champions said to be bores grows whenever nothing can be found to criticise their achievements. Boring; hmm, in a world obsessed with trivia would it be better if Phelps had been found 'roasting' in the Olympic Village? Is it not enough that he is the best ever in his field? Why should a super-talented sportsman also be a raconteur?

Most lamely, Phelps's diet was pilloried. He eats 12,000 calories a day and some of it is junk food! That he needs so much fuel did not register with the critics, most of them looking as though they matched his intake but hadn't walked a step in two years. In fact, Phelps's diet merely proves you can eat almost what you want if you get off your sniggering backside, instead of wallowing on the sideline mocking those who don't just talk.

Truly British; truly pathetic.

Steven Gerrard innocent until proved otherwise

January 2009

Many years ago I was in a posh London pub with two other England rugby players. We were just chatting when a bloke lurched past one of them and shoved a bit of paper at me, saying, ''Ere, sign this.'

I told him he could at least say please, having spilt the player's drink. It wasn't haughty to ask for the basic courtesy, but he replied, 'Oh, I have to say please now, do I? Who do you think you are? Too good to sign, are you?'

I signed and handed the paper back. He looked at it and said, 'What do you call that?' Running out of patience, I told him I had done as asked, but was having a drink with my mates and wished him goodnight, whereupon he squared up to me.

What do you do? Do you continue to take the further abuse he gave, or do you front up? I would have fronted up were it not for the fact that several years earlier in a Nottingham pub, after the third time someone had a go at me, I snapped and hit him. I should not have done, but I did and still I think he deserved it.

There followed a section 47 charge and sentence.

I don't know any of the Steven Gerrard alleged assault details. He is innocent until proved otherwise, but I know how anyone can be stretched beyond normal endurance.

Matt Stevens has my best wishes

January 2009

I admire Matt Stevens; not for letting down his closest and leaving England short, but for his candid admission of a drugs illness and his guilt under sporting laws. This was against present practice of blaming somebody else for spiking your drink/conning you/not protecting you.

Stevens took the risk, got caught, should get punished and banned.

A double standard exists in the treatment of athletes and entertainers using 'recreational' drugs, but there is no other way. Attempts to distinguish performance- and non-performance-enhancing drugs would lead to judgements capable of exploitation by lawyers for those using the latter.

All the interviews I have heard asked what effect this would have on his club, Bath, and their players. His employers have expressed a feeling of betrayal; not so fellow players. They will care only about Stevens's recovery.

Rugby has not reached the point where players have many clubs in a career. A large number stay at one for good. This allows deeper relationships to develop and with more intimacy comes empathy. That Stevens plays as a prop is also significant. When you rely on the performance of two other men for your physical wellbeing, it engenders even deeper solidarity.

Your stance on this depends on whether you accept Stevens has an illness. This is the impasse between addicts and non-addicts, sympathisers (not apologists) and non-sympathisers. To the latter this is a lack of willpower, thus not an illness, thus there is no sympathy.

The former, or those intimate therewith, believe it is a question of strong self-will tragically misdirected. They are, or have been, 'driven' high achievers unable to explain their inability to stop doing what they know risks all. Illness then visits. It is not invited – thus the visited attract sympathy.

None of this is helped by the celebrities who check into rehab as a PR stunt.

Stevens now finds himself selected for the biggest of all games: one for his life. He can count on my support.

25

I'm hooked on motorcycling

January 2009

There are no half-measures when it comes to being a biker; there is no room for indifference. Once you have experienced the exhilarating acceleration, made more real for not being insulated by the protective shell of a car, you're either hooked or know it's not for you.

For more than forty years I was in the 'can't see the point' camp. Cold, insular and dangerous were the three words that described my estimation of motorbikes and I never made a serious step towards two wheels.

Only by dint of necessity did I get to try this second-class transportation. As the BBC's MotoGP producer, my wife used two wheels to commute. When she became pregnant she decided not to ride and took the car, leaving me transportless, other than the vile public transport I had suffered for eighteen years and wanted no more of.

The first lurches on a beginner's 125cc around a tennis court did not portend what would transpire. Passing my Compulsory Basic Training released me on to a small scooter, which would accelerate away from all but the most committed and powerful cars, could filter to the head of queues and was just so energising.

Using a standard Honda CB500 for my full licence revealed what joy could be had with more power. Simultaneously exhilarating and terrifying, the addictive thrust of merely turning your right wrist gripped me and has not yet let go. It's no exaggeration to call me obsessed and I admit that part of the elation is the tinge of danger ever-present when only protective armour lies between you and the road.

There is, however, nothing thrilling about the inattention of other motorists. Assuming the worst of any vehicle waiting to emerge is vital to provide the best chance of avoiding injury. Although my riding career is short, that assumption has saved me three times – from a woman in a 4x4, smoking and using her mobile; a cyclist shooting a red light; and a white van man who I am convinced saw me but didn't care. This peripheral awareness has also made me a better driver – how many times do you look in your wing mirrors before turning?

I cannot deny the stupid riding of some bikers and it is probably a good thing that I did not pass my test when I was eighteen years old and feeling invulnerable. Having done, as a solicitor, a good number of catastrophic personal injury cases involving bikers, I know one incident is enough to paralyse.

To satiate my lust for speed I did my first track day at Brands Hatch with the excellent Focused Events team recently. Only by track riding do you get any estimation (and that's all it is) of the skill of professional riders. The chance to ride knowing that whatever you do there isn't going to be a lorry coming the other way is priceless, as is the fact that if you do slide and fall you will not hit a kerb or a lamp post.

After my instructor had watched a few laps of me riding in a group his first comment was 'You're quite aggressive, aren't you?' Is it that obvious? I didn't think so. My line into the corner is mine, that's all.

I thought I had leant into the corners as far as was possible and yet he said there was another 20 per cent to go. In genuine trepidation I flung myself over in the next corner and it held. I had got my knee down. That sounds like nothing but it was genuinely as thrilling as running out at Twickenham.

Okay, it's not as much fun in bad weather, but you just wrap up. You can't have a six-CD changer system, but you feel alive because the bike's performance is physically linked to you, as opposed to your right foot.

Me, I'm hooked.

26

Gouging is cynical, and plain cowardly

January 2009

In the uber-violent world that was French club rugby in the late 1980s there was a requirement for most front row players to wear a cricket box. They weren't afraid of one unexpectedly rearing up off a length, rather that the opposite hooker was about to swing on his props and plant both feet on their crown jewels.

This was not the only manifestation of foul play that ran through the French game. Gouging has been an ever-present, but I remember one game when, as a spectator, I saw the whole menu used.

Agen were playing Valence d'Agen, their bitter local rivals, and there was trouble from the first ball. At the line-out, Philippe Sella drove the ball forward at centre. The Agen forwards drove over him and the ball was then moved away. Three opposition forwards held Sella down and when everyone else had gone proceeded to give him a hiding.

When the Agen forwards realised their deified captain was in trouble they turned and ran to help. The first player to arrive launched a two-footed drop kick into the jaw of one of the assailants. There then followed a pitched battle; none of your handbags at dawn but a fully blown fight using feet, elbows, heads and the usual fists.

The referee dismissed the drop kicker, but was helpless for the rest of the half as ten all-out brawls took place. At one point the referee sin-binned two forwards from each side, leaving five and six others, respectively, to play on. When the ten-minute suspensions were up and the four players returned, two of them started scrapping immediately. They were both dismissed, but resumed fighting in the tunnel and had to be separated by police.

To its great credit the French Rugby Federation used swingeing bans to stop the violence which had spread to the national side. These were the days when you could ruck players from the breakdown and stop them killing the ball. Nobody has ever, as far as I'm aware, explained why this practice was so wrong that it had to be shunned in favour of a system which too often produces slow ball. It may be because, as with most things, a small number of players took this chance to dish out pain in general.

Later in my career, whenever I played against Wales I would wear a 'reverse' shinpad. This protected against the then penchant for treading on a player's calf while ostensibly only rucking him away from the ball. This target was selected because if the foot was planted effectively there was nothing a player could do. His calf would swell, then seize and eventually he'd have to leave the field.

Gouging has gone in and out of 'favour' but was prevalent in the late eighties and early nineties. Many times against France I suffered, sometimes so blatantly it can clearly be seen on camera.

The increased number of cameras has led to the decline in foul play at top level and rightly so. Kicks, knees, elbows and punches are invariably spotted by touch judges; where not, the operation of a post-fact citing system allows retrospective punishment.

But gouging has made an unwelcome return in recent months. The latest incarnation involves an allegation against Leicester prop Julian White on a Welsh opponent from Cardiff on Saturday. If proven, White faces and should be given a lengthy ban.

I think the reason for a raised number of gouging allegations is that, with most other things being caught, it remains one of few acts of foul play that is difficult to spot.

However, of all acts, gouging is the most cynical, clinical, callous and cowardly. Further, it is the one which can leave irreparable damage to the most important of the five senses. Anything which makes its presence less likely should be used. Mind you, if they feel weaponless, players could try the perversely premeditated foul play of Australian Rugby League's John Hopoate.

After one game three North Queensland players claimed that during tackles Hopoate had tried to ram a finger up their anus in an attempt to make a quick 'play-the-ball'. Once this claim was public, several of Hopoate's previous opponents came forward saying this had happened to them, but they had been too embarrassed to mention it.

The hearing before the NRL judiciary is available on the internet but I warn you not to read this while holding a hot drink, or any similar substance which, if spilt, might cause injury. If you can desist from convulsing for a few seconds you will see that Hopoate's case, presented by a QC, no less, was that he had been merely trying to administer that favourite schoolboy pranks, the 'wedgie'. Quite why that was appropriate for a first-grade game is not clear.

Hopoate was officially found guilty of 'unsportsmanlike interference'. As one witness said, 'I was disgusted. I know it's a tough game, but there's no room for that.'

27

St Moritz's 'Racing on Ice' is a unique sporting festival

February 2009

The minute-by-minute landing of Learjets in St Moritz this weekend will give a hint that the 'Racing on Ice' meeting is no ordinary get-together.

Having played in the 'Cricket on Ice' tournament that precedes this festival, I can tell you that it is extraordinary, not only for the preternatural combination of horse racing and snow, but also the gathering of Europe's über-wealthy.

At such an event, discussions about the quality of the powder do not necessarily relate to conditions on and off piste.

Any tightening of belts will be the Versace belts of the various examples of 'mutton dressed as mutton' parading about, festooned with a variety of dead animals and gems. Any surgeon specialising in Botox therapy should be on the next available flight.

The actual racing is fantastically different; spectacular and bewildering concurrently. The cricket precursor less so, though its spectacle will depend on the seriousness with which its participants have approached St Moritz's legendary nightlife.

It is rumoured that after one such night David Gower's car sank imperceptibly through the ice, leaving a difficult call to the hire company.

As a committed member of Robin Smith's XI, my only runs came as a result of the inability of the opposition wicketkeeper to gather the ball while convulsed on the floor at my missing the ball by at least a foot and then trying not to vomit while running the byes.

Robin had no such difficulties, belting the ball to all points. This ability, he told me, stemmed from the fact that he often batted for England while in a similar state, following nights out with Messrs Botham and Lamb.

I declined my invitation to do the Cresta Run on only one hour's sleep, though that seemed not to bother Allan Lamb, a veteran of both this danger-filled thrill and sleep deprivation.

I opted for curling with a mate, who failed to understand that the stone is released gently, not like ten-pin bowling. We watched, he with gathering horror, I with gathering hysterics, as his stone gained speed over the ice, finally skipping over the edge and through the windscreen of a parked Mercedes.

That the owner would be an inductee into the famous book of *Unbelievable Insurance Claims* was probably of little comfort.

If you can get there, go; there is no festival like it.

28

Giles Clarke should carry the can for Sir Allen Stanford shambles

February 2009

Background

Sir Allen Stanford was a Texas-based multimillionaire whose first foray into cricket was organising a tournament for high prize money in the West Indies.

In June 2008, Stanford and the England and Wales Cricket Board (ECB) signed a deal for five Twenty20 internationals between England and a West Indies all-star XI with a total prize fund of £12.27 million to be awarded to the winning team (West Indies).

The deals were set to revolutionise cricket with talk of a truly global game, though many within the game were not happy about the haste with which the ECB embraced Stanford.

On 17 February 2009, news surfaced of an $8 billion 'massive fraud' investigation by the US Securities and Exchange Commission. As a result the ECB withdrew from talks with Stanford on sponsorship and on 20 February severed all ties.

Whatever your view of the state of Test cricket, the news that Sir Allen Stanford is now charged with an $8 billion investment fraud by authorities in the United States is probably not going to make you leap out of the bath with a Victor Meldrew-like shout of 'I don't believe it!'

To be fair, nothing has been proven, but are many of you

genuinely surprised that something of this ilk has surfaced, particularly as the cricket boards of India and South Africa reportedly refused to deal with him. Surely that should have rung alarm bells.

It is not as if Stanford did not come without baggage. ECB chairman Giles Clarke states that they were aware of the money Stanford had put into West Indian cricket and that encouraged the England and Wales Cricket Board to deal with him.

How many times have those of you who are parents found yourself saying, 'Yes, and if they stick their hands in boiling water, do you do that as well?'

One of two things seems to have happened, and neither is good enough.

The first, which is the more likely to me, is that, in the face of the sheer panic caused by the creation of the Indian Premier League and threats of player revolt, county backlash and the like, very little proper due diligence was done into either the man or his business background, reliance being given to the flimsiest of recommendations.

Alternatively, which is far worse, this potential business tie-up was the subject of proper and detailed scrutiny, and the results were ignored, again because of the overriding pressures of the IPL.

The ECB, in the words of Clarke, would like to move on. I'll bet they would, but we are again at a juncture where somebody ought to be carrying the can. Stanford would probably pass the football test about suitability, which seemingly welcomes anybody, even if they are human rights' abusers or torturers, but is this really good enough for cricket?

Last week, I said that Hugh Morris should resign as managing director of the England team. I feel even more strongly that Clarke should go, not just because of the Stanford affair, but for the unseemly panic over the IPL, and the fact that he still does not seem to want to find out who leaked Kevin Pietersen's views on Peter Moores.

29

Should Sir Jackie Stewart take public money?

February 2009

A contract is a contract, says Sir Jackie Stewart, who has had a mixed response over his refusal to relinquish his £1 million per year as an ambassador for the Royal Bank of Scotland.

Before discussing the ethics of Stewart's stance, the fact that RBS on Wednesday pulled out of their deal with Williams means we should ask what RBS were doing in Formula One in the first place. The Six Nations sponsorship makes sense as it is, and was, RBS's home market, but this dive into a notoriously expensive sport was always more questionable. Further, given that many of the companies owned by RBS were not specifically rebranded as RBS property, the effectiveness of such a generic deal was in doubt.

You have to ask who on earth gave Stewart such a beanfeast in the first place, and was any part of the deal performance related?

Now, Sir Jackie has unquestionably been a great servant to Formula One, but it would be interesting to see if any analysis has been done to see if the same – or more – profit has been earned through work he has done, though this is notoriously difficult as cause and effect in this sort of business-getting role is often intangible.

Stewart's refusal would be acceptable were he simply dealing with a multinational private company. He is not. There is a clear distinction between taking advantage of a deal made with a private business and taking money from taxpayers who have had no say in whether they wished their money to be committed to rescuing RBS in the first place.

Some say that as the RBS executives refuse to forego their bonuses, Stewart may do likewise. This is a flawed argument; if you reverse the two, you are saying that because Stewart refuses to give up his contract the executives are justified in doing likewise. Just because some act avariciously does not make it right for others to emulate them.

Stewart is not a poor man and he has the opportunity to mirror the wise decision of fellow Scot Andy Murray in renegotiating a far lower package, taking less taxpayers' cash once the extent of the Government bail-out of RBS became clear

Should he not do this, he deserves the same opprobrium heaped on RBS top management.

30

ECB are wasting money hiring head-hunters to help find a new coach

February 2009

The England and Wales Cricket Board have appointed Odgers Ray & Berndtson, an executive 'head-hunting' firm, to obtain the views of thirty-eight of cricket's finest about who should be appointed the next England coach.

An enormous fee will now be paid for essentially the recording and distillation of pages of interview notes. From what specialist standpoint will the author of the eventual recommendation differentiate between, and give weight to, the hundreds of points made by those interviewed?

If the ECB claim that they will use the recommendation only as a guide and will exercise their own discretion, what is the point of the head-hunters?

An advert on the ECB's website states that the new coach will be expected to promote 'the highest standards of behaviour and discipline'. I presume that means he should not consort with people facing allegations of fraud and links with drugs cartels, not leak confidential documents and be prepared to be sacked without doing much wrong.

Hugh Morris, the director of England cricket who is the 'appointer', claims the move will ensure an open, transparent and objective process and, by using a third party, he can introduce extra rigour. Conveniently, it also provides another party who can be blamed should the appointment prove to be a mistake.

They are believed to be the first organisation to take this step. Why are the ECB doing it? It should not be necessary in a competent governing body who accept their responsibilities.

The ECB are also spending yet more money on lawyers to advise whether there is a case to be made against the Professional Cricketers' Association. The ECB believe the PCA wrongly claimed that they leant on their chief executive, Sean Morris, to increase the pressure on the England players during the Test to sign a revised agreement with Sir Allen Stanford.

The ECB claim that, far from warning against their ongoing involvement with Stanford, the PCA were arguing that he should be held to his original contract.

Under what branch of the law will they claim: defamation, breach of confidentiality, breach of contract?

So far as defamation is concerned, to succeed a claimant must have a reputation to protect. Given the ECB's recent blunders, they may find establishing this a tad difficult.

Then there is confidentiality. 'M'Lud, I refer you to the Pietersen precedent and the maxim: those who seek equity must do equity.'

And, finally, breach of contract – as worthy as the paper on which it is not written.

This action is a waste of members' money and contrasts in its vigour with the inertia over uncovering who breached his duty of utmost good faith in leaking the Pietersen report.

Moreover, since when were the PCA the governing body for English cricket?

The final paragraph of the opinion will advise there are some grounds for action, but against this must be weighed a number of inconsistent facts making a successful claim far from certain – oh, and that will be £100k, please.

31

My love for football makes its faults so maddening

February 2009

From the age of six I went with my uncle, Gladney Robinson, to the Shay to watch Halifax Town. My friends supported Leeds, Manchester United and Liverpool; I shouted for Alex Smith, Terry Shanahan and Micky Kennedy.

It is easy to follow big clubs; with a Fourth Division team you have to savour small victories. I saw Halifax beat both Manchester United 2–1 (Watney Cup) and City 1–0 (FA Cup). The first when Alex Smith saved a Willie Morgan penalty, the second when the Halifax players were hypnotised by Romark the Magician before stepping on to a quagmire; Paul Hendrie scored the only goal of a game Malcolm Allison later decried as a farce. The following year Halifax, under Alan Ball Snr, went up to the dizzy heights of the Third Division. In 1971 Halifax finished one place short of promotion – having been to nearly every home game I was sick as.

These memories are vivid, being novel experiences. The iconic theme tune of *Sports Report*; the local *Green Final*; never winning the golden goal and what passed for hooliganism at Halifax – Mad Bob of the Skircoat End. I only later understood why the white-coated man selling prawns, mussels, whelks and kippers attracted ubiquitous shouts of ''Ave yer got crabs?'

Though it is not a stellar achievement, I played No. 9 for the Halifax Under-11 team, three of which later signed forms. Given the single-minded, almost pathological verve with which I pursued a rugby career, I honestly believe I could have played football professionally in the lowest league.

When eleven, I went to a rugby school and from then on played rugby nearly every Saturday for the next twenty-five years; though physically unable to watch football, I followed it avidly on TV throughout that time.

I returned to watching football due to being sent off (twice in eighteen years) and banned for nine weeks for treading on an opponent, one of few players to get dismissed while possessing the ball.

I went to Stamford Bridge and watched Ruud Gullit's team in full flow; well, almost. The tribal atmosphere, the rawness of the crowd and live football excited me the way it had when I was young. The next year I bought a season ticket and have done so every season to date.

At the first game of the season you discover who you will have to listen to all year. Mine wasn't a good start; the guy next to me came out with these two rib-ticklers: 'It's the wrong shaped ball for you', and 'Just remember, if they use their hands – it's a free-kick.' Where was Mad Bob when you needed him?

I quickly realised I watch games in a different way from most fans, at least at Chelsea. Countless hours of player, team and tactical analysis means that I rarely watch the ball directly. Premier League football live lets you marvel at the speed of players; the little space and time within which they work; the fitness, agility and the ingenuity of the most gifted.

You may disbelieve all this, given the stick I regularly dish out to the nation's favourite game. Yet it is for that precise reason that it attracts my admonishment. Something that has the influence of football should be run as well as possible; setting standards, not reflecting the lowest common denominator. That football has hitherto been a working-class game is no excuse for the substandard; that argument would never be run in relation to education.

Experience from another sport gives me the advantage of not accepting accepted football practice. So I ask: why is it accepted that a player cannot use both feet? Why do they, and why are they allowed to cheat, dive and feign injury? Why is the FA's Respect campaign not being fully implemented at the highest levels of the game and sanctions made against those who weekly undermine its aims?

As I do not have to 'keep in' with anybody in the football world to provide me with stories, I can ask questions about corporate governance issues, particularly the ludicrously lax 'fitness' quali-fication for club owners.

This sounds unutterably arrogant – it is not meant to be, it is just that I know other sports have things that would benefit foot-ball enormously, the use of technology, the ten-yard rule and the sin bin being examples. I know that players and fans can eschew vileness and I will not accept that 'football is different/more pas-sionate' rubbish.

Relatively minor changes in administration, rules, and attitude, would make football what it purports to be; thus, it, its managers, players and fans would get the respect they believe they are owed as of right.

What right have I to comment on football? I love it; what more do I need?

32

Paul Gascoigne's on the right road

February 2009

Paul Gascoigne's most recent interview with a national newspaper shows nothing new, other than the context.

Gascoigne faces the same issues that have dogged him since his teens. He shows the same flaws and the same strengths. As such, further repetition should be dull, but it is far from that.

Each interview, as Gascoigne battles against addiction, reveals a step towards the point where the man can recover.

The most recent and significant development was Gascoigne's statement that he has to recover for himself; not his family, friends, or the public.

As only he can do the work needed, he now has the right focal point.

Comment (May 2010)

Gazza, as he became known, may have a life that turns out to be a Shakespearean tragedy, in the true sense: an untimely death at the end of an inexorable series of linked events – some of which have been magnificent – all ultimately stemming from his idiosyncrasies and flaws.

His is one of few sporting autobiographies (done with Hunter Davies) that is worth reading, but if you focus on the man and not his achievements and exploits there is revealed a person who from his early years has had psychiatric problems.

The signs are classic – morbidity before the age of ten; obsessive compulsive disorder in his teens; addiction and obsession in his football career – they are all there. That they went either undiagnosed or untreated early is more than a shame because, had the reverse been the case, Gazza might now be passing his undoubted footballing genius to a succession of English kids.

There are numerous reasons for Gazza's non-treatment, some more acceptable than others. A natural antipathy within his family and wider community towards any sort of 'shrink' ensured he did not go beyond an exploratory consultation with a child psychologist.

Next came his extraordinary progress through football's junior ranks, which turned into a professional career when he was still below majority age. What could be wrong with him if he could do all this? Anyway, he's just a bit daft.

Sport's multiple benefits sometimes mask problems like Gazza's; compulsive training is laudable; obsession with statistics or rituals is seen as quirky, but not sinister. Gazza is not alone in being able to disguise problems through excessive dedication to training and playing, and his football career had enough signs of developing illness, but in the midst of international football and celebrity they were ignored and not necessarily purposefully. For him and those around him it must have seemed that there were not enough hours in the day to accommodate all who wanted his involvement.

His earlier mental illness would not have made his slide into addiction inevitable, but it would predispose him to it. Add this to the unusual psychological challenges that fame, fortune and retirement bring and you would not even have got a price from a bookie on this coming to pass.

The traditional view that Gazza's addictions led to mental illness is, to me, incorrect and the wrong way round. As addiction was his first illness to receive substantive treatment and publicity, many assume his subsequent problems flow therefrom. In fact, various disassociated psychological problems like those listed above were present long before addiction, but this seems to have got lost somewhere in the whole saga.

Gazza's well-publicised twelve-step treatment was part of treating his manifest addictions but it was only ever going to be a partial solution to his problems. It is sometimes said that an addict is not responsible for his illness but once it is diagnosed he is responsible for his recovery when he gets treatment. This may be so with normal people but those like Gazza with extra mental problems are unlikely to succeed on such programmes without other treatment and possibly drugs to arrest the onset of different psychiatric disorders.

What is illuminating is the changing view of the public as his illnesses progressed. Initially there was widespread condemnation, as there is when high-profile and successful people are reported to have addiction problems or depression. What has he got to feel sorry about; snap out of it; it's only a matter of will. These are just some of the comments that flew his way.

It was not until he was admitted to a 'proper' mental institution, as opposed to one of those celebrity treatment centres, that he was given the benefit of the doubt and people began to accept he was ill. In addition, the disturbing sight of a once athletic figure looking unnaturally aged made it more real for many because they could see the effects of his illness.

Perhaps now the limelight is being withdrawn and he gets treatment for all his ills he may get a chance to write another story. In public he may say he has already lived a glorious tale, and compared to ordinary people he is right. Quietly and when he is more lucid, he will know that it could have been even more glorious, but he does not owe us that; he owes us nothing. He owes himself much more, but as he has found out, when it comes to repaying those debts it is infinitely more difficult.

33

As Dwain Chambers publishes, athletics is damned

March 2009

Dwain Chambers defies logic; not his enhanced performances on the track, but the whole issue that now blights UK athletics by his continued involvement in the sport.

His recent book serialisation in a national newspaper has dragged into the limelight other figures who have no control over the maelstrom that now engulfs them as a result of being mentioned by Chambers.

Sebastian Coe, Christine Ohuruogu, Rio Ferdinand and John Regis, his former agent – who is threatening legal action over claims he knew Chambers was on drugs – are all featured in the book *Race Against Me*.

The problem with Chambers is the wider question that applies to crime and punishment. An offender is convicted and sentenced according to the offence; once served, he has paid his dues.

That there will be a residual stigma is inevitable, and most people would support the notion that a person should be able to pursue a useful life after punishment. Had this been the intent, surely it would have been part of the original sentence.

This is the logical and intellectually fair stance and yet it hardly ever applies consistently to any offender; sometimes because of the offence, sometimes because of circumstance and often due to nothing other than fortune. Most find employment difficult to obtain and few will be allowed to return to their former careers; they may be forced to move to find a new life.

This background is set out to put into context the claims made by Chambers that he is the victim of hypocrisy and double standards. I presume that he believes that having done his time he should be free to pursue his former career with no impediment.

Chambers, who still has a six-figure debt, is fortunate that he is immediately able to resume his career and take part in lucrative meetings if he performs sufficiently well. A lawyer, doctor or teacher would almost certainly not be given this privilege.

Further, the offence which led to Chambers's ban was the most fundamental crime in sport – drug-taking. It was not bad behaviour on a night out or an unconnected offence; it was a strike at the heart of competition, whereby all are supposed to start from the same point.

Chambers's complaint about a bar being placed on possible selection for an Olympic Games is also not especially weighty.

First of all, governing bodies must have the right to select on criteria which are fair. If they are consistent and also disbar anybody else banned in the same circumstances as Chambers they are not being discriminatory.

That some athletes have been subject to lesser penalties does not automatically place them in the same category as Chambers and thus the selection criteria can be different without being unfair.

Secondly, Chambers has been allowed to return to his employment and is free to earn therefrom. The Olympics does not attract prize money: therefore how has Chambers been prevented from earning his living? You may assert that from Olympic success come endorsements and indirect earnings. You may, or may not, be right, because all such are hypothetical and cannot be equated to prize money fixed for any particular meeting.

On a different point, Chambers may well have been accepted back into the athletics fold had he not striven to keep his name in highlights. He has to accept that by maintaining such a profile he will alienate some people.

Chambers berates the authorities for not following his allegedly sound allegations concerning the timing of drug offending, and his hints at where might be found other cheating athletes. However, he will not name names. On his sole word the rest of athletics is damned; how can you trust a word the man says?

34

Greatness is still unproven for Ireland's euphoric Grand Slam winners

March 2009

This is a consequence of my own experience, but I am finding it hard to mirror the utter euphoria that is engulfing the Emerald Isle, where partying to match the events of the revelation to John is taking place.

I understand the significance of the sixty-one years, but having won three Grand Slams I, perhaps, have a more measured view than the Irish faithful about where their team sits in the pantheon of great sides. Furthermore, I understand that the emotions of the Irish players will not be uniform and to some surprising.

That the deciding game was an epic contest is not in doubt; the shuddering commitment of both sides, the drama of a last-minute missed penalty and two wonderful minutes for Ireland that produced fourteen points. It was a great finale.

Ireland overcame the numerous penalties awarded, rightly, against them and in this they showed a firmness of belief that sets them apart from their Irish predecessors. Their coach, Declan Kidney, has at last managed to fuse the hitherto warring factions from Munster and Leinster into a team that is the sum of their parts.

In achieving this, Kidney has transparently utilised the footballing and social skills of men from either province, captain Brian O'Driscoll (Leinster) and pack leader Paul O'Connell (Munster).

Both players are touted as suitable to captain the British and Irish Lions' forthcoming tour to South Africa and my choice would be O'Connell because where he plays, the second row, is in the heart of the most important battle for the Lions, which will be, first and last, up front.

O'Driscoll's description of the dressing-room scenes after the final whistle were familiar to me, but not the expected and easily recognisable emotions of joy and excitement; more when he used the words 'relief' and 'satisfaction'. Players of his talent and experience, those who have gone through the crushing experience of failing to win decisive games, carry with them a barely concealed dread of repeating the experience. When this spectre is lifted, it is more exorcism than excitement. The real pleasure for the older players will come this week as the achievement is reinforced by the reception they will receive in every part of Ireland, including, no doubt, the parade of Dublin which is sure to be offered.

On O'Connell's part, I am sure he will concur with my comment that the sheer physical attrition to which an international forward commits himself tinges any celebration with exhaustion, but in the end gives a sense of inner satisfaction that cannot be beaten. What is also known by players like Ronan O'Gara and those of similar vintage is that this achievement has to be contextualised within world rugby, another level to which they have at times ascended, only to be demoted very quickly. Young players, those not experienced in the World Cup, will see this as the only game in town because they have not had the exposure to a higher level of international rugby.

So, cheers for a very good, but not yet great, Irish side; back-to-back Grand Slams are rare and if Ireland repeat this year's feat they then deserve a place at the table of greatness.

The statistics place England second in the tournament and the leading try-scorers, which seemed unlikely before the competition. As pleased as Martin Johnson will be with these two facts, he will not be satisfied and nor should he be. England's first forty minutes of Saturday's Calcutta Cup were confident, and, though they ran in tries, they should have put the game to bed, given the number of times they won good-quality ball in Scotland's twenty-two. Nevertheless, all the England backs were in the game, providing options and dummy runners inside and outside. It is possible to see pattern and shape within the England performances. Although they may not dominate for eighty minutes, this is the nature of proper Test matches; the secret being to capitalise on your periods of dominance.

Johnson has the right venue for his summer workout in a tour to Argentina. He has to keep the team progressing. Unfortunately, I cannot see progress with Scotland. I do not mean that they have not competed well; their problem remains unaltered – they cannot score tries and produce momentum because of their failure to execute basic skills in the contact and the final pass. I am not sure how much further Frank Hadden can take this team; he simply does not have enough raw materials.

Finally, spare a thought for Wales, and the sporadic periods of the total rugby they alone in the northern hemisphere play. They failed to hit the heights and their challenge is to find the consistency shown by great teams.

Roll on South Africa, though, unfortunately, I see a possible whitewash there – and not to the Lions.

Postscript

To illustrate my point about the difficulty of a country achieving successive Grand Slams, Ireland finished second in the 2010 tournament, having lost to both Scotland and France, themselves Grand Slam winners. In both of these games the Irish had a fifteen-minute spell during which they did not concentrate and were made to pay for it. They could have won both games, but in the end found that such small periods of inattention are enough to shatter the highest expectations; that is why the list of double-slammers is so short.

35

Tennis wasting Wimbledon's wealth

March 2009

A management consultant will tell you that any goals you set must be realistic and agreed by all concerned, and that if targets are not pragmatic they are highly likely to be missed, causing resentment and disappointment.

Two years ago, the Lawn Tennis Association president, Stuart Smith, said Britain should have five top 100 players by the end of 2008. Roger Draper, the LTA chief executive, recently admitted that this was not likely to happen until 2010, but claimed, 'They were the wrong targets in the first place. Those were the targets set in the old strategy.' Draper insisted he had never been working to the target.

My God, this sport cannot even agree to which plan it works and the resultant goals. Although the failure of the LTA is accepted as readily as increased rail fares, the outcome is far worse.

To appreciate fully how badly the present and past managers of British tennis have failed, you need to look at the sport itself and its position *vis-à-vis* other minority sports.

The overwhelming complaint of most minority sports is that they are starved of cash, forced to rely on unpaid volunteers and living hand-to-mouth.

Tennis, because of Wimbledon, has never suffered these privations. It is rich in comparison. Profits from Wimbledon since

1997 have hardly ever dipped below £30 million and when the LTA decided to build a National Tennis Centre in Roehampton, the £39 million was readily available.

A close second in the list of disadvantages comes lack of exposure. Women's football and rugby, both far more successful than tennis, complain constantly about this. Tennis does not have this problem.

For two weeks every year, leaving aside for a moment the week before's build-up, tennis has the number one tournament in the world at Wimbledon. No other sport has such comprehensive coverage of an annual tournament.

Approximately ten hours every day, on TV (terrestrial), radio, internet, iPlayer and mobile phone, are devoted to tennis in SW19. About 13.1 million people watched the Rafael Nadal v. Roger Federer final last year. If you compare that pro rata with the coverage of football's World Cup and the Olympic Games, held once every four years, it actually receives greater coverage than both.

Also, the blanket coverage in all national newspapers, independent radio stations and specialist publications creates a publicity machine for which any minority sport would sell its soul.

Even outside the Wimbledon tournament, tennis is incredibly well served by the huge TV coverage from British Eurosport and Sky Sports.

Although there have not been many, tennis cannot either claim it has not had high-profile British players. From Virginia Wade, Jo Durie and Annabel Croft to Tim Henman, Greg Rusedski and now Andy Murray, it has not lacked a would-be star that people could identify.

Schools participation is a problem, but no more than with other sports, and the amount of land required for tennis is significantly less than football, rugby or cricket.

The cost of participation in terms of equipment is relatively low. A decent racket costs no more than the latest Nike trainers and fees at the local municipal courts are not high. Moreover, there are few areas that do not have some facilities.

Against this background, the failure of tennis and the LTA is an utter scandal. It has most of what other minority sports lack and it still cannot get its act together. Unfortunately, the reason for this, apart from the incompetence of its governors, is that it is stuck with a middle-class image that emanates from the snotty All England Lawn Tennis and Croquet Club, which permeates through local clubs and alienates those who are 'not the right sort of people'.

36

Sepp Blatter and football are wrong to reject new anti-doping rule

March 2009

So, football has rejected the World Anti-Doping Agency's (Wada) 'athlete whereabouts' rule, specifically drawn up after wide-ranging consultation with most sports.

Many other sports have embraced this as a necessary evil; not because they all have rampant drug-cheat problems, but because they recognise their responsibilities to sport in general, knowing that uniform standards send the most effective message to would-be cheats.

In Britain, testing body UK Sport's plan is for thirty elite players to undergo up to five tests a year – not including those conducted after matches.

Footballers believe the new rule, under which athletes have to inform testers of their daily whereabouts, is an invasion of their privacy. Brussels-based sports lawyer Kristof de Saedeleer, acting on behalf of a number of sportspeople, including footballers, has likened the system 'to putting a whole town in prison to catch one criminal'.

Sepp Blatter, the FIFA president, who also sits on Wada's board, states: 'FIFA and UEFA want to draw attention to the fact that the legality of the lack of respect of the private life of players, a fundamental element of individual liberty, can be questioned.

'It is not a question of not fighting doping, but one should not really go for witch-hunting because witch-hunting has never led to a positive result. FIFA and UEFA wish to point out the fundamental differences between an individual athlete, who trains on his own, and a team-sport athlete, who is present at the stadium six days out of seven, and thus easy to locate.'

Blatter claims that FIFA's stance is supported by other team sports, including basketball, volleyball, ice hockey and rugby union. The Professional Footballers' Association, unsurprisingly, is opposed to the Wada rule and their chief executive, Gordon Taylor, said, 'We feel to invade the privacy of a player's home is a step too far.

'We do appreciate that football is a major spectator sport and we wish to cooperate, but football should not be treated in the same way as individual sports that do have a problem with drugs, such as athletics, cycling and weightlifting.'

Superficially, as with most of the things the above people say, there appears to be merit in their argument; alas, yet again, a modicum of forensic scrutiny suggests otherwise.

First of all let us disabuse ourselves of the notion that this requirement is fantastically onerous. It applies to only thirty players per annum; so the suggestion that it will affect all Gordon Taylor's members is nonsense. I would also presume that having been in this group for a year a player will then be exempt from being so for a prolonged period.

We must also consider what the regulations state, as opposed to the impression that those trying to avoid such scrutiny would have us believe.

This is about all that is required: the thirty players have to specify one sixty-minute slot between 6 a.m. and 11 p.m. each day where they will be available for testing at a specific location. This slot may be during any team activity (individual or group) conducted on the day in question.

If, as Gordon Taylor asserts, footballers are more often than not at their clubs all they have to do is say that is where they will be. Is this difficult? No. Prison-like? No.

Moreover, the above renders the request for a collective location rule otiose. It also does not invade a player's home as he can specify another location, including his club stadium. As for demonising these proposals as a 'witch-hunt' – this comment belongs in the 'Stupid Things Said by Stupid People' box wherein Blatter's 'football is slavery' rubbish already resides.

The deliberate attempt at disassociation by naming sports known to have drugs issues is lame. Football is not dissimilar to many team sports that have adopted these regulations. Moreover, Blatter's claim that rugby union supports his stance is simply wrong. International Rugby Board Regulation 21 Anti-Doping adopts the Wada stipulations and was adopted by the Rugby Football Union, coming into force on 1 January 2009.

Of course the emotive issue of family holidays has been played for all it's worth, but on this I proffer the words of John Fahey, the president of Wada:

'One of the key principles of efficient doping control is the surprise effect and the possibility to test an athlete without advance notice on a 365-day basis.

'Alleging, as FIFA and UEFA do, that testing should only take place at training grounds and not during holiday periods, ignores the reality of doping in sport. Experience has demonstrated that athletes who cheat seize every opportunity to do so and dope when they believe they won't be tested.

'Some substances and methods disappear quickly from the body while keeping their performance-enhancing effects. Anti-doping organisations must therefore be able to test athletes at all times in an intelligent fashion.'

As for Blatter's boast that 'every year, the footballing world organises between 25,000 and 30,000 doping controls and is committed to fighting doping in football with all of its means', given that there must be about 60,000 professional and semi-professional footballers worldwide this equates to one test every two years per player.

Just why does football think it is entitled to differential treatment? As an Olympic sport, the game will be obliged to comply with the Wada code and perhaps the bad publicity of expulsion would concentrate the minds of football's rulers. This appears to be the only language they understand.

I simply wonder this: given the uniquely powerful position of football, the huge rewards for many of its players, its potential to lead for the good of sport; even if these regulations were onerous, which they transparently are not, would it not show a great example to the rest of the sporting world if football embraced this standard even though the probability is that it does not have a widespread drugs problem?

No, as all too often, football is content to plough its own furrow, leaving itself open to unwelcome accusations that it must have something to hide or that its players are all prima donnas. Why FIFA, UEFA and the PFA are happy for this image to linger, when the resolution is so simple, is bewildering.

37

ELVs' zealots are a law unto themselves

March 2009

On Monday and Tuesday the International Rugby Board meet at the picturesque Lensbury Club, Teddington. As they debate rugby's Experimental Law Variations (ELVs) they should consider why the area is so beautiful.

In the 1960s, against the fad for all things modern, the local authorities and residents were derided as old-fashioned for not embracing changes in planning and style; they bore jibes of being out of touch and had they not done so the landscape would have irretrievably shattered.

Nobody has identified what crushing blight existed in rugby in 2003, apart from England winning the World Cup, which demanded thirty-five ELVs. The game was successful and attendances and audiences growing. Even so, in they came, without widespread consultation; and ever since, all manner of invention, threats and abuse has been used by their proponents. Unfortunately, I have not space for detailed dismantling of the bad ELVs. There are some which are beneficial, but let me set out things as they were and are, and not how some wish to assert.

The only rationale given for this exercise when it started was to remove the random element from the game, allowing players, not referees, to decide matches. It was said too many kickable penalties were winning games as opposed to tries; note, no mention of freeing up the game or making it more attractive.

If this were a properly run test, discussion would be limited solely to whether the randomness has been removed/lessened.

As IRB figures show, very few international games are won by the side scoring the fewest number of tries; *ergo*, teams cannot rely on the referee's arm to win by playing negatively and forcing penalties; *ergo*, the whole premise was flawed as framed.

Even though strictly we should not even be discussing such points, the number of penalties and free-kicks combined under the ELVs shows referees intervening more, not less. Moreover, the decision to be made by a referee as to whether an act was intentional introduces the most subjective and, in fact, impossible judgement.

Debate soon changed, without official explanation, from 'randomness' to the hyper-subjective assessment of whether the game is more attractive under the ELVs. Such concepts are incapable of standard definition; there is no objective 'right' or 'wrong'.

Criticism, especially from the southern hemisphere, has been thrown at anyone, especially from the northern hemisphere, who questions what they claim are transparently beneficial improvements.

Generalisations portray anyone complaining about aspects of the ELVs as being against any change. The very terminology used to portray anyone who dares to demur has been skewed, caricaturing those with differing opinions as, variously, Neanderthal, old-fashioned or out of touch. Change is given the benefit of descriptions like advancement, improvement and so on, as if any change has the right to such.

This is illogical: it is perfectly possible for inertia to be beneficial and an improvement, if the alternative is poorer. It is the same fallacy as the claim of the current Government concerning the present economic crisis, that 'doing nothing is not an option'.

Comically, today's games that are exciting are down to the ELVs; those not so are due to inadequate teams; selective attribution is intellectually dishonest. Anyway, there were brilliant, and poor, games under the old laws.

As it appears we can debate tangentially to the original premise, is there more or less space during play under the ELVs? There
is less, and how is this beneficial? The mind-numbing homo-
geneity of endless pick and drives has replaced the art (for that is
what it was) of the maul; which drew in players, but does so no
longer as it can be pulled down immediately. Of any change this
is the most blatantly stupid and damaging; its removal and the
reintroduction of law 20 requiring a straight scrum feed would
disproportionately improve the present fare.

Finally, the most disingenuous and thus most objectionable
ploy perpetrated by the proponents of the ELVs is to say that
those opposed 'do not understand rugby'.

We do understand, we just do not agree.

This claim is the last refuge of many a Turner Prize winner, dis-
missing criticism of their pile of rubbish as not being true art. It
is the last desperate defence against those who see the emperor's
new clothes for what they really are.

As I have been held up as one of those least understanding,
especially by the Australian journalist Spiro Zavos, I ask this: who
is likely to have a greater understanding of the game – someone
who has played schoolboy, university, students, Under-23, B,
junior club, senior club, divisional, Hong Kong Sevens, international, British Lions, Five Nations and World Cup rugby; who has
played and won, home and away, against every major international
board country, or someone who may have played a bit and
watched a lot?

Finally for the IRB: rugby has always been a players' game;
please keep it so and not the bauble of couch potatoes and the
self-interested.

The opinion of any third team player counts more than that of
a spectator, even if they have a platform or a marketing degree.

38

Good riddance to the ELVs – never again

April 2009

'Ding, dong, the witch is dead' is the refrain from all the little people.

All but two substantive law changes have been sent to the abyss. From conception to abortion, the law-change experiment has been a ghoulish farce which has harmed the image of rugby. That it caused mirth from other sports is not as important as the fact that it caused active hatred between genuine supporters of the game. This sort of destabilising and divisive exercise must never happen again.

Any law variations attempted in the future should have strict criteria for their introduction, framing, trialling and evaluation.

The International Rugby Board's internal group with the nebulous brief to 'improve the game' should be disbanded or given stricter guidelines. At present, and similar to the Commission for Racial Equality, they have to find problems in order to exist; with the Experimental Law Variations they did just that.

Any future change must specify the precise evil which it intends to address; and, where possible, have supporting statistical evidence. This requirement alone would have stopped the ELV fiasco even starting. The IRB's own, undisputed international statistics irrefutably proved that the claim that teams were winning on penalties rather than tries was simply not true. It is astonishing that nobody thought it necessary to check this properly before embarking on a course that caused two years of misery and ultimately failed.

If such a need is identified a precise description must be made of what is being addressed and what will be the criteria on which it will be judged. This will stop interested parties trying to use phrases like 'more open', by which they mean any definition of this impossibly subjective phrase that suits them.

Having defined as tightly as possible what is being done, the IRB then has to ensure that it is done uniformly. I have said this many times – no product, drug, law or similar would be allowed without it being trialled over the same period, in the same trial conditions and using the same trial subjects. Any future trials must be unanimously accepted, or, if passed by the majority, must be uniformly imposed.

Finally, the evaluation of the recent ELVs was one of the most ridiculously partial processes ever. After only a few days of the first trials the self-interested IRB were briefing for their pet laws. This continued unabated until the IRB finally voted; indeed, in the case of the laws sent back for further consideration it continues in the same fashion. They were joined at various times by high-profile figures in the administrations of various Unions, particularly Australia and New Zealand, who were then aided by a compliant press corps. The Orwellian sophistry from Anzac journalists has been astonishing; the fact they cannot see even the slightest possibility that they have acted in such a way is quite chilling.

Can you imagine the furore if those who test products interfered with the testing process; if they went round making biased assertions about interim results and publicly tried to alter the framework in which the tests were considered?

The IRB should also tell us what this whole farrago has cost. They won't, of course, because when the time of everyone in the Law Project Group, other IRB people and their counterparts in all the Unions worldwide and the associated expenses, including those of the globe-trotting bias merchants, are totalled, the figure must be millions.

When they do sort out the laws process I have an urgent matter for them to consider. The breakdown, statistically and by perception, yields the most penalties and causes referees, players and spectators the most difficulty of any part of rugby.

In the Six Nations the BBC replayed an incident when Paul O'Connell, the Irish second row who tackled an opponent without releasing either the man or the ball got to his feet, tried to take the ball he had never in fact released, shouted, 'Referee, he's holding on', and got the penalty. It could have been any international forward who drew that penalty. Only in slow motion is it possible to spot this gamesmanship without guessing and it is only going to get worse.

The only solution I can see is to prevent the tackler playing the ball at all, making supporting players responsible for winning the ball, thereby committing at least one more player to the breakdown.

How about then making it even easier for referees and saying that nobody can play that ball with their hand until it has been won? Referees would then not have to decide at what stage a player had put his hand on the ball legally and when a ruck had formed and he had to let go and so on. In fact, apart from the ban on the tackler, go back to the law that used to prevent all these difficulties.

39

Andy Farrell's retirement will mark the passing of a rugby legend

April 2009

In the early nineties, Will Carling, Rob Andrew and I went for a drink to discuss developments in the then England players' campaign against the Rugby Football Union over its refusal to implement changes to the amateur laws.

To our immense surprise, stood at the bar were three rugby league players, one of whom was Andy Farrell. I was more than curious about their presence in a Barnes pub overlooking the Thames, though I suppose it offered a better vista than the Manchester Ship Canal. More curiosity was caused by Farrell's beige-coloured leather jacket that looked as if it had been lifted from the set of seventies television series *Starsky and Hutch*.

After a good fifteen minutes of uncomfortable glancing at each other like people in a nightclub, Kris Radlinski was eventually the first to speak and we all chatted guardedly for a while before making our excuses and going our separate ways. I was later told they had been for a meeting with the RFU about switching codes, though, unusually, I have not been able to find any confirmation of this.

It is difficult today to understand the divide that existed in those days between the codes of league and union, though this was created by administrators, not players. Present players would have no difficulty in each other's company, but not then. Farrell was the least communicative; I think he thought we were all southern jessies, even though I was from Halifax.

I criticised the RFU's assisted purchase of Farrell from Wigan in March 2005 because I thought that at his age then, nearly thirty, it was too late for him to acquire the different skill sets required in union. His car crash and other injuries prevented him from making his debut for Saracens until 2006 and his subsequent England career was not the success his advocates had predicted it would be. I was also critical of the selectors for prolonging his stay in the team, which I said would not have been done had the RFU not been invested so heavily in his career.

When I met Farrell recently, instead of the cool, if not hostile, reception I expected, he spoke frankly and warmly. I should have remembered what a man and what a professional he was. More than anybody else, his standards meant that he knew that he had not been the success he wanted to be in union.

His retirement at the end of this season should be marked as the passing of an extraordinary career. Farrell's league record is a litany of 'the youngest' . . . senior first-team debut at sixteen; winner of the Challenge Cup aged seventeen years eleven months; full international at eighteen and Player of the Year in 1994.

He left league with the following incredible record: five championships and four Challenge Cups with Wigan, the 1998 Super League and 2002 Challenge Cup as captain; three thousand points in all competitions at Wigan; the Golden Boot as the best player in the world in 2004, the Man of Steel Award twice, and the Players' Player Award; second in the list of England's all-time goalscorers and second in the list of England's all-time point scorers.

That Farrell added only eight England union caps to this glittering record does not mean that he did not have the talent to succeed in union; I believe it was only down to a matter of timing.

Farrell will not bow out to the fanfare afforded some rugby players. This is a shame, and, making no distinction between the two codes, I salute him as one of the very best.

40

Stamford Bridge classic revealed football's good and bad sides

April 2009

Tuesday's astonishing Champions League quarter-final second leg between Chelsea and Liverpool at Stamford Bridge had all the elements, both good and bad, that make this level of football compelling and distasteful in equal measure.

Watching from the vantage point of a supporter, sat close to the home/away fan divide in the Shed End, as opposed to from the press box, simply served to intensify these experiences and all football journalists should occasionally eschew the cosy confines of their press room and attendant seats for a reacquaintance with such rawness.

First let's get the ugliness out of the way.

One man nearby had the temerity to have a ticket in the wrong section. He may have done this purposefully, though I doubt it, as he sat making no noise even when Liverpool surged into a two-goal lead against a Chelsea team mired in stupor. The spotting of a red hat in his pocket kicked off his manhandling by fans and ejection from his seat. He had to run up the aisle and out of the section accompanied by punches, some connecting, others missing.

My revulsion at the fact that it is not possible for a person to sit with opposition fans without risking assault will confirm to many 'true' fans that I am not one of them; so be it. I prefer to inhabit a world in which such things are possible, as indeed they are in most sports.

The continuation of Didier Drogba's maddening oscillation between being the physical scourge of central defenders and Oscar-nominated actor for best feigned injury has become a joke, even to die-hard Chelsea fans. It now draws only shouts of 'get up' and opprobrium of a more prosaic nature.

The excitement, and it was truly thus, was largely the result of inexcusably poor defending from both sides and both goalkeepers having bouts of the yips that matched Bernhard Langer's putting. All of which led to the taunting between the rival factions being alternately defiant and triumphant.

This is part of the game and some of it was humorous; however, much of it was bigoted and without any wit or intelligence. The notion that, post-Taylor Report, the football landscape is all sweetness and light is illusory.

What did absorb was the willingness of both teams to attack, something that the five previous meetings in this tournament I have watched at Stamford Bridge painfully lacked. It also saw the players and managers at their best in one respect – indomitability.

The surges of disappointment and hope that accompanied every goal could easily have debilitated some competitors, but neither side quit.

In addition, the goals scored from medium-range free-kicks by Fábio Aurélio and Alex were shining examples of, first, inventiveness and then sheer power. The performances of Frank Lampard and Xabi Alonso were masterclasses in the art of midfield play.

The added spectacle of John Terry and Steven Gerrard, their respective team's spiritual and official leaders, sitting in the stands provided another delicious irony.

As each goal led to a close-up of their reactions, delight and disappointment were obvious manifestations, but the subtle undercurrent of helplessness and the quelling of passion that they showed in glimpses were a more entertaining behavioural study than thousands of hours of *Big Brother*.

When football hits these notes it is irresistible.

41

Usain Bolt's admission no bolt from the blue

April 2009

The 'news' that Usain Bolt recently admitted to knowing as a child how to roll a joint belongs in the same category as the fact that bears defecate in woods.

Given its role in Jamaican and Rastafarian culture, it would only be surprising if Bolt did not know how to do this.

Equally predictable was the apology forthcoming from Bolt to the Jamaican people for the fact that his earlier comment might have led to the opinion that all Jamaican kids know how to skin up.

This hasty clarification probably came after advice from PR people, but only in the present climate of political correctness would this be so.

People are actually capable of seeing a little humour and a tad of exaggeration in Bolt's offhand remarks, without their minds jumping to such ridiculous generalisations.

That Bolt does not take marijuana himself is clear, which is not good news for his fellow athletes, because Lord knows how much slower he would run when giggling hysterically, or after eating the entire contents of his fridge.

42

Fabio Capello's focus on respect highlights football's low standards

April 2009

The various words of Frank Lampard, the Chelsea and England midfielder, featured heavily on the sports pages two days ago. His comments were interesting for a number of reasons because they give an insight into the previous and present mindset of both England management and players.

Fabio Capello has reformed the dress code, insisted on respect for hotel staff and guests, made the team eat together and banned mobiles while they dine, and removed the WAGs. Lampard believes these alterations have lifted the squad and, together with Capello's tactical nous, have created a situation where 'we all trust him'.

Good: anything that helps these individual talents fulfil their promise as a team is welcome.

However, many other sports and players therein will concur about the necessity of tactical perception, but will maintain their wry smiles that both football players and journalists think that the other matters are revolutionary. The very fact that they have been the subject of comment raises questions regarding the Football Association, the Premier League and players themselves.

Capello's rules are so basic that it is astonishing they are thought remarkable. Furthermore, this necessarily means that more than one of his predecessors failed to correct, or possibly even address, these basics. What does this say about the standard of coaching and management in England?

What does it say about the FA's choice of managers if they have not insisted on the sort of standards that other sports require as a minimum? What does it say about the Premier League system which creates players to whom these changes are a 'slight culture shock'? The only thing shocking is the shock itself.

The most telling comment about Capello's way is that the players have the perception that he picks on form. Detailed scrutiny might provide anomalies, but perception is sufficient to create true competition. All players, of whatever level, are prepared to accept selection on this basis, even though they might not be happy, because it provides evidence that extraordinary effort will be recognised.

Many managers recognise the effects of such an approach and state it to be also their way, only then to do the contrary. The difference that can be made by consistent adherence to this tenet is starkly illustrated by the contrasting fortunes of Clive Woodward's 2003 World Cup winners and his 2005 Lions losers.

Lampard's comments about the new-found selflessness of England players to the joint cause illustrate that Capello has seen and dealt with previously selfish play. This issue is difficult and exists in all sport; do you pick the system and make the players comply; or the reverse? Capello has got it right.

Another tick on Capello's report card should be his handling of Wayne Rooney. Not only has he specified for him an effective role that allows him to shine, but he has refused to agree with another widely held piece of football rubbish – that if you in any way temper Rooney's lunatic tinge, he is thereby neutered. From Capello has come rebuke, not excuse, and Rooney's attitude under the Italian is proof that understanding a little less and condemning a little more is the right way.

Having posed the tangential question as to why is it that the England players have not themselves recognised and rectified the facile behavioural points above, there is at least a partial rationale in Lampard's comments about the young players of today – 'They have it too easy.'

This comment might be the football equivalent of the rant made by many a talk-show caller about society. They could just be because Lampard, like all of us, is getting older. What is different and worrying is what Lampard prescribes as a remedy – cleaning boots. This is such an unreconstructed cliché, but unfortunately there will be thousands, maybe more, who nodded in agreement.

It is claimed such menial work reinforces discipline, reminds the cleaner of his lowly status and gets him used to graft. All of these things are also achieved by making young players get a proper education; in fact, the concentration and dedication required to study is infinitely more taxing than shoe-shining; all the more so, as for many young players it will mean confronting learning difficulties that they have previously been allowed to ignore because of their sporting promise.

And what have the kids learnt after they do their 'Lampard time'? Even if they do learn the values claimed, they are no wiser; they have not been given any new resource with which to face the consequences of any subsequent success. Is it not obvious that education is so needed and would be so beneficial to both football and footballers?

43

Boris Johnson's school playing field numbers fail to add up

April 2009

Should anybody doubt the seriousness with which Boris Johnson, the Mayor of London, approaches sport, they should listen to what he says and does. On Tuesday he was again extolling the virtues of sport, albeit in his rather eccentric way. Why, he has even appointed Kate Hoey, the former Minister for Sport, as his Commissioner for Sport. However, a little examination of the background to Johnson's policies and their effect on London sport suggests more talk than beneficial action and not much prospect of improvements in future.

The Mayor has given the go-ahead for a redevelopment of Holland Park Community School in west London, in the teeth of strident opposition from local council tax payers. The sale of 1½ acres of playing fields, it is claimed, will fund 20 per cent more outdoor space, sports pitches, an Olympic-size indoor swimming pool and a gymnasium, which will all be available for use by the local community outside school hours.

Johnson said, 'Local children will now get a school fit for the twenty-first century which will accommodate an extra one hundred school places in the future. This scheme will also increase space for outdoor sports and other activities.'

These figures are disputed by residents who claim that the school will provide only thirty additional spaces at a cost of selling off 1½ acres of playing fields (25 per cent of the site) and losing more than 50 per cent of the habitat areas which will be concreted over. The telling verbal gymnastic vault is in the mention of mere sports pitches, which is not a commitment that such will be maintained at their previous level. Furthermore, indoor sports facilities are no substitute for full-sized sports pitches.

As for Hoey's introduction, the move creates yet another layer of bureaucracy in the crowded area of sport funding. At some point, the study of the annual cost of delivering taxpayers' money and lottery cash will reveal the true extent of all this paper-pushing and how much it takes away from athletes and general sports enthusiasts.

At least Hoey has overcome some of her previous reservations about the mayoral office and the Olympics. Before the election of Johnson she said there should be a debate about 'just how the Mayor's functions are working, because I think for a lot of people there's a feeling that the Mayor perhaps is a kind of elected dictator'. A job offer seems to have settled that conundrum.

The conversion to the cause of the 2012 Olympics is even more Damascus-like given her strident opposition to London's bid; she supported the French bid for Paris.

At least we have to hope that her involvement does not end in anything like the Wembley farce which was substantially delayed while the Government dithered about whether there had to be a running track included in the scheme. The delays caused by such procrastination nearly derailed the whole project and added to the cost.

Driving the personality out of sport
Given David Coulthard's assessment of the percentage contributions to a win in Formula One as 80:20 (car and driver), how does any F1 driver ever get voted Sports Personality of the Year? Even when athletes take enhancing drugs, it is still 100 per cent their body, training and performance.

Robbie Savage's performance on Radio 5 Live was a breath of fresh air

May 2009

Radio 5 Live's football coverage this week included as a co-commentator a player who would be nobody's selection in a list of the top ten most articulate footballers (if that is not an oxymoron) – Robbie Savage. However, his observations and thoughts made during the Aston Villa v. Hull match were entertaining, direct and refreshing; a mile away from Sir Trevor Brooking's ubiquitous 'Well, I'm sure he wishes he'd done better.'

Savage's musings were made in the accent and language of the very common man, but this did not matter because he added colour and insight and was not afraid to be direct about fellow professionals when he thought it was justified. Surely it will not be long before he takes his place in the BBC's *Match of the Day* panel.

The only blip in his performance was his admission that he did not know the offside rule. However, in this ignorance he is not alone and it is astonishing how many of his professional colleagues, their managers and many commentators and pundits do not bother to acquaint themselves with what is a relatively simple rule, even if its application causes problems and disagreement.

Give Joey Barton a break or Premier League circus will just make him worse

May 2009

Joey Barton's long-term recovery from various illnesses or defects of moral character (depending on your point of view) stands little chance of succeeding while he further subjects himself to the pressured environment of Premier League football. It is an atmosphere he is demonstrably unable to handle. Whether or not his indefinite suspension from Newcastle is seen by others as the just deserts of an ill-tempered oaf does not matter; however it is described, it is in his best interests.

The essence of sport is competition, if not conflict, more so when it is the livelihood of the participants. Add to this the presence of tens of thousands of committed supporters, the scrutiny of television, radio and other forms of media and you have a situation that challenges those players who have rationality and experience. The occasional sins of players such as David Beckham, Steven Gerrard and the like attest to the fact that such demands can make the best player do regretful things.

When these stresses are visited upon a person with obvious frailties, there is never going to be a happy outcome until the demons that revel in chaos are neutered; they will never be removed permanently.

Barton should have sufficient money to secure his future, but he will not have one unless he removes himself for whatever period is deemed necessary by those trying to help him. The professional judgement of organisations such as the Sporting Chance Clinic will not involve any consideration of the forthcoming season and it is essential that Barton is now guided by their advice, rather than that of his agent, or any manager or coach.

In doing this he will also stop his colleagues having to deal with a litany of inevitable questions about his future, popularity or lack thereof; in short, matters which should not be visited upon them. He has to be made to recognise that he is not the only person affected by his behaviour.

Nobody now can say what Barton's footballing future will be. It could be that he does not have one, but his sanity is more important. If this means he does not play at this, or any, level again, it is a price worth paying – ask Paul Gascoigne.

In contrast, consider Sir Alex Ferguson. The many accolades given to him principally address his phenomenal footballing achievements; no better displayed than in Tuesday night's demolition of Arsène Wenger's Arsenal in the semi-final second leg of the Champions League. Yet on top of this, he deserves to have added praise for his personal courage in being able to focus on the job in hand despite his daughter-in-law and grandchildren being injured in a car crash earlier in the day.

Any parent or near relative will confirm that during such times of trial this kind of anxiety can make concentration almost impossible as the emotions cloud the thoughts. That Ferguson was able to conduct himself with focused dignity could, to some, be the sign of coldness, almost inhumanity, but his passion is well known. Therefore, this control, exactly the opposite of that shown by Barton, is a mark of his character, not a character defect.

46

Formula One's warring factions are making the sport a laughing stock

May 2009

Any sport has to have a ruling body which sets the rules and enforces them. If the participants do not like it they should work within the rules and use the procedures to effect a change of personnel that will reflect their desires – if they can persuade enough people to back their proposals. In return, the ruling body has to be competent and look after the interests of the sport itself, not any individual concern, however large, and certainly must not govern in its or someone else's own interests.

New regulations introduced by the FIA, Formula One's ruling body, have two main stipulations. First, a voluntary £40 million budget cap. Second, greater technical freedom to those teams which choose to adhere to this cap on spending. These proposals are supported by luminaries such as former world champion Niki Lauda and the smaller teams which have regularly been handicapped in their contest against high-spending major teams such as Ferrari, McLaren, Renault and Toyota.

The righteous indignation of several of these teams to the FIA's attempts to make the sport more interesting and responsive to the present economic climate is predictable, repetitious and boring. *Déjà vu* of *déjà vu* is the impression of most sports fans.

By now most people understand that this is about power: the ongoing and long-running conflict involving Bernie Ecclestone, the FIA and the major corporations that now form the Formula One Teams Association.

The opposing sides are now making F1 a complete joke, if it is not so already, and they are culpable when it comes to their operations and the way in which they go about getting what they want.

No credible sporting hierarchy takes out anything near that which is garnered by commercial rights holders Ecclestone and CVC Partners, nor forces through decisions made solely on whether they allow this huge bounty to continue.

It is transparently not in the interests of anybody, other than the aforementioned entities, to take out nearly half of a sport's profit, unless the vast majority of that money is redirected into the development of the sport at all levels.

A competent ruling body does not switch venues from those that attract spectators to those that do not, then compensates for this by the presence of broadcasters. It does not make its prices eye-wateringly expensive for ordinary people. It does not pursue a deliberate divide-and-rule policy which prevents teams legitimately opposing the things that they do which are not in the interests of the sport and which are made solely for gain. It has transparent and fair disciplinary structures.

These are legitimate complaints, and yet the major teams now griping about the latest issues have not had the guts to openly confront these excesses. Part of the reason for this subservient compliance is that the major manufacturers are happy with the permitted imbalance, which hitherto has allowed them to out-spend their rivals. They have not stood up and championed the causes of increased competition and a fairer deal for the smaller manufacturers. Nor have they seriously tried to limit their spending when not faced with economic difficulties. The Jacks have been all right up till now.

If the battle were being fought on these grounds there would be room for much sympathy for the teams. However, the issues on which they have chosen to fight and the methods they have adopted are disingenuous and trite.

Ferrari, who have been allowed, against all definitions of fairness, to compete while possessing concessionary 'guaranteed rights', are the worst offenders. Relying on the slavish devotion of their fans, they threaten to quit, on the assumption that their supporters will no longer participate. Really? The fact that they religiously watch lap after lap after lap of this worldwide snoreathon, anticipating the occasional overtaking manoeuvre or bungled pit-stop, demonstrates a level of commitment bordering on the maniacal. In the face of this addiction it is highly unlikely that they would completely forego their fix.

Although Ferrari are willing to ignore the basic tenet of any sport, that no individual or team is bigger than the sport itself, they should consider what it gets out of the whole relationship. The success of F1 worldwide marketing through their presence is undisputed. Where else are they going to ply their trade that has anything like the global exposure that F1 affords them? While many people cannot see what the fuss is about, the petrol-heads from all manner of countries obviously do get it and consequently make deluded purchases of cars, in the belief that in some way the possession of something shiny and red makes them a better human being.

Moreover, the achievements of Lewis Hamilton and Jenson Button are the reason for the viewing figures of the BBC's F1 coverage. The public do not care which car brings British driving success; they just want winners. The same goes for all other countries, save perhaps Italy itself.

The fact that other major manufacturers have piled in behind Ferrari in order to better their own and not the sport's best interests merely compounds the shame.

The wearing effect of all these mêlées is now beyond a joke. High-spending manufacturers should not make routine withdrawal threats – how much are their brands devalued by them rightly being seen as bullying whingers?

For F1 to have any credibility, if there is any left anyway, one of two things has to happen.

The FIA has to say 'Close the door behind you' at this public blackmail; a governing body should not permit itself to be bullied in this way. F1 got over the loss of Lotus, Ligier and Brabham, and it will get over the loss of one or two major teams – not that they will act on the threats anyway.

Alternatively, all the manufacturers have to take concerted action to prevent Ecclestone and the FIA ruling the roost, by setting up their own championship, but one which promotes greater competition, more excitement and maximises the influence of the drivers, as opposed to the technicians, on the result.

The chances of either are so remote that F1 should not whinge if most people wish a plague on both their houses.

47

England v. Andorra: London tube strike is good for sport. Honest

June 2009

Background

In December 2003 the RMT called a strike because one of their members was dismissed after being caught playing squash while being on sick leave. Over the years many more strikes were called and another was set to begin on 9 June 2009 which would have affected the England football international at Wembley the following day.

Mr Bob Crow of the National Union of Rail, Maritime and Transport Workers (sic) clearly loves sport. It appears that whenever possible he and his members want to bring particular events or minority sports to the public consciousness, giving them much-needed column inches and reminding us that it is possible to use sport to achieve wider aims in life.

Take the previous case of Crow's defence of the right to play the under-publicised game of squash. So important did Crow deem the right to play this game that he was willing to risk public opprobrium to support one of his members who was being victimised for the mere sin of playing a few harmless games while on sick leave.

In similar fashion, Crow has over the last two days given a timely reminder both of the Government's excellent initiative to get more people to walk at least a few steps each day and of the multiple health gains brought by exercise.

The RMT's latest supportive action, which Crow reminds us in a statement on the RMT website has not been taken lightly, shows Crow's inventive backing of the Football Association. On Wednesday night thousands of England fans, parents and young children will have enjoyed walking the few miles to see the World Cup qualifying game against Andorra at Wembley, as opposed to the crowded and sometimes dangerous journey by tube.

They will have been reassured of the wisdom of the FA's decision to buck the example of other countries by retaining a national stadium and siting it for the convenience of the majority of its fans.

Such is the selfless dedication of Crow to sport that we can certainly expect further initiatives during the 2012 Olympics. The public will, no doubt, be assisted in seeing, close up and on foot, the regeneration of east London wrought by the billion-pound investments of council tax and fare-paying Londoners.

As if all this were not enough, can we forget Crow's amusing anecdotes about his support of Millwall FC? Perhaps he could explain to the lads down there that the £1 million refund given to England fans who could not get to the game last night by the FA is just another example of greedy owners and management intent on denying ordinary folk and their families much needed funding for grass-roots sport.

He could add, while he is at it, that there is always collateral damage during strife, though he may find squaring this with the hitherto demonstrated love of sport more difficult.

48

Wimbledon 2009: Andy Murray offers a genuine contrast to the All England Club

June 2009

It is almost time for the annual invasion of SW19 by Margot Leadbetter clones. They come, resplendent with Union Jack bowler hats, substituting for a moment support of their slim-limbed favourite tennis player in place of badgering the local council about the state of the street lighting outside their gated communities.

This year will be even better: the sparkling new Centre Court roof awaits. To be fair, it does look good. They also have the prospect of cheering for somebody who might actually win. Previous antipathy towards Andy Murray for anti-English comments has rightly been put away because of a number of admirable things done by the Scot. His admission that his remarks were foolish helped, but, more than that, his offer to accept reduced money from one of his benefactors, Royal Bank of Scotland, was unprompted and immediate, in contrast with the slower response from Sir Jackie Stewart.

More than all this, Murray has been winning. Style matters to some, but it should never be preferred over triumph and Murray's progression through the tennis rankings is down to honest graft. And Murray's candour in defeat is refreshing in these days of the scripted sound bite.

Murray aside, the contrast between state-of-the-art playing

surfaces and arenas is stark when the seemingly never-to-be-ended failure of the Lawn Tennis Association, via the All England Lawn Tennis and Croquet Club, is considered. No change in the offensively elite membership scheme for the most exclusive enclave in Britain. As they maintain, they would have to give out more tickets if there were more members – can you believe this offensive rubbish is still publicly stated?

Visitors to the official Wimbledon website may be misled by the reference to 'The Long-Term Plan'. Naively, they may believe this is the latest in a series of Grand Plans to try to get at least more than two players into the top-fifty ranked players in the world.

Not so; it relates to that which is much more important: improving facilities to be the best in the world. This does also improve facilities for the-less-than five hundred members, but to point this out is unpatriotic.

No; player development, they say, is down to the Lawn Tennis Association, whose top bods last year could not even agree to which plan they had been working; they all rub their hands and say, 'Well, never mind, it all looks so lovely.' The tone is set by the All England Club and Keeping Up Appearances isn't the right one.

I don't think I will go. As I live only a mile from the grounds, I will be able to hear most of the women players' shrieks and screams indoors. The breathing used to aid effort, for example in weightlifting, is short and sharp, timed to coincide with the effort; anything longer is unnecessary and affected. It is cheating and should be stopped. Not least so that I can sit in the garden in peace and have a cold one.

49

Sport England should do what it says on the tin

June 2009

The revelation by the *Daily Telegraph* that Sport England has possibly allowed millions of pounds to be doled out without ensuring accounting regularities were regular comes as no surprise to me. A few years back I was unexpectedly invited to an interview to sit on its board. Scheduled for forty-five minutes, my chat lasted barely twenty. Possibly my level of charm and decorum was limited, but they knew that anyway. It was probably the words that gave me away.

The interviewing panel misunderstood my reply to their clichéd inquiry – what makes you think you should be on the Board of Sport England? When I said I should be given the job because I didn't desperately want to do it, they must have thought me indifferent. What I meant was that I didn't see the post as another part of a CV, another notch on the way to the Honours List; nor was I interested in sitting and chatting, without doing.

I also addressed their scepticism about my conflict of interest as a journalist and confidentiality. It was perhaps not wise to snort and express incredulity, saying that Sport England had leaked like a colander for years, or to question the wisdom of the question by pointing out that if such things were written by me I could hardly then deny being the leaker, attributing to an unknown, inside source.

However, what I think finally did it for me was my reaction, in front of representatives from the Department for Culture, Media and Sport, to Government (not just this one) attitudes to sport. Firmly atop a tall soap box, I couldn't help but let rip. Why was there not a Department for Sport and a permanent place in Cabinet? Money for sport is supposed to be for that; not to supplement the health service budget, trying to make fat, indolent people at least walk from their sofas to turn over the TV manually once a week.

Sport is sport, not mild exercise. Sport England was not defending properly the funds for organised sport. I could not forget a conversation with local PE teachers, only weeks before, wherein they informed me that organised sport was, in many schools, still not properly carried out and that 'cooperative' exercises did indeed exist instead of school sports days. Whatever they told me, and whatever they told everyone else, was not accurate.

A Department of Sport combining those parts of the DCMS involved with sport and some of Sport England would be more effective, cheaper and directly accountable. Until a party creates such a department, its avowed love of sport is hollow. And while we are at it, the increasing costs of this body, inquiries and all, divert money that could and should be spent on, ironically, sport. Is this too simple?

50

Lions 2009: Bryce Lawrence
not fit to officiate

June 2009

Background

A short explanation is required to put this article in context. The first Test ended with a Springbok victory by 26–21, but it was not achieved in the way expected. The Lions were taken apart in the set piece and especially the scrums in which they had fielded an experienced front row. So comprehensive was their dominance that the Springboks ran up a lead which they held despite a furious recovery from the Lions.

Phil Vickery of England, at tight head, faced Tendai Mtawarira, nicknamed 'the Beast', at loose head for South Africa. Before that Test, Mtawarira was not noted for his powerful scrummaging; it was his bullocking runs in loose play that earned him that nomenclature.

To the untrained eye the Beast simply ragged Vickery at will and at one point had him under so much pressure that Vickery was lifted five feet in the air, for which he was penalised by Bryce Lawrence, the Kiwi referee, for standing up.

The Beast did not repeat his dominance in the second half and could not do so in the remaining Tests. How, then, did he stuff a World Cup-winning and hugely respected player? Simple: he was allowed to scrummage illegally by Lawrence.

Although the Lions did not convert a number of chances which would have won them the game, there is no doubt that the foundation of South Africa's first-half dominance came from the scrum. I am not suggesting the Lions would have won but for this issue, nor am I denigrating the Springbok victory; but what I am saying is that we should not have to face such suppositions and that was Lawrence's fault.

In the second Test, Lawrence was an assistant referee running the touchline. In the opening minutes he saw the South African flanker Schalk Burger put his fingers in the region of the eyes of Lion's winger Luke Fitzgerald. The referee was unsighted but his attention was drawn by Lawrence who recommended 'at least a yellow card' for Burger. Even from the footage captured by cameras that were further away than Lawrence, Burger was guilty of gouging which warranted a straight red card.

Burger received ten minutes in the sin bin and the Springboks went on to win the Test 28–25 and established an unassailable lead in the series.

As a postscript, the ludicrously lenient six-week ban dealt out to Burger after the game proved Lawrence's recommendation was wrong and the subsequent bans on players for offences that were no worse than Burgers (up to seventy weeks) shows the disciplinary committee were also wrong and both brought the game into disrepute worldwide.

In the face of a second defeat by South Africa on Saturday, the British and Irish Lions players and management have tried to maintain that most British of things, a stiff upper lip. In the best, but outdated, traditions of stoicism, and probably for fear of being called whingers, they held back from saying things as they are.

Sometimes this approach is laudable, but on this occasion it was not and rugby is done no favours by cowing any criticism of matters that are of the gravest concern. 'It's a man's game'; 'if you can't stand the heat'; blah, blah, blah; bring down as many of these pathetic validations as you like, but sensible people need not resort to cliché when faced with irrefutable evidence of nefariousness. To the victor go the spoils, but not the right to rewrite matters as wanted. In Test rugby, the least wanted aspects of professionalism are appearing – spin, refusal to answer or pose direct questions and sophistry. Rugby needs none of these but is slowly being enveloped.

Refereeing is difficult. Referees deserve our support. In return, they and their governors have to front up when things go badly wrong and not seek the shelter of another cliché – that, without them, we would have no game; as if their contribution is some form of community service out of which they get nothing. Well, without us they would have no game either. It is correct that decisions open to interpretation under rugby's complex laws are only the subject of discussion as opposed to vilification and censure, but sometimes it is not right to turn away for risk of causing offence.

The man who has cost the Lions dear, in not one but both Test games, is Bryce Lawrence of New Zealand. We are not here talking about whether a pass was forward. His serious errors are incapable of rationalisation, save by the misapplication of the tenet that a referee is the sole arbiter of fact and law. That stipulation is intended to allow referees to be wrong, not stupid.

If Lawrence, as touch judge, is incapable of linking the vileness of an act occurring two feet away and the proper sanction of a red card, he is not fit to officiate. No argument. No 'it happened in the first minute'. It is wrong. To add to this failure has to be his otherworldly view of Phil Vickery, rammed five feet off his feet, then penalised for an illegal act in the previous Test.

Does Lawrence, the referee then, know why lifting is illegal? Is he familiar with hyperextension of the spine? How did 'the Beast' curiously dominate, then capitulate? The previous week he was allowed to cheat with impunity; two days ago he was not. Simple, really.

Nobody with a vestige of sanity in rugby excuses gouging the uniquely vulnerable and valuable soft tissue of the eyes. It is rightly seen as the cheapest of shots, cowardly and potentially career-threatening. Schalk Burger, IRB Player of the Year recently, will have had to explain an act so far below the standards of a player who deservedly won that honour.

Peter De Villiers, the South African coach, commented that Burger did not deserve even a yellow card because other things were missed and it was all part of the game.

Back on planet Earth I have to ask this: how far out of whack is De Villiers's sense of right and wrong to even think such things, never mind say them at a press conference? The heinousness of this act was highlighted by John Smit, the Springboks captain, when he directed there be no more questions about it.

Of the rugby, most of it was played by the Lions. Platitudes and moral victories will mean nothing to the players; they know that they had sufficient possession and chances to win both games. What they must allow is the fact that no team can realistically expect to accommodate seamlessly the loss of all its first-choice props and centres during a Test of this intensity. Nobody doubts their courage: it is littered about the fields of both Tests; but, similarly, no one can doubt the South Africans' mental toughness and ability to take chances when they arise. Their first two tries were the product of scrupulous analysis of the Lions' defensive patterns; the absence of a receiver at the line-out was brilliantly exploited in their riposte to an early Lions try.

Less noteworthy was the Springboks' repetition of the casual violence visited on England a few years ago when their then captain referred to his player's concussion and asked, 'Do you think he did that to himself?' It was meant to be a rhetorical question and indeed it very nearly was – the player was knocked out by a punch from a team-mate.

That such undesirable issues draw as much coverage as 160

minutes of pulsating, sometimes infuriating, often mesmerising, rugby is unfortunate, but not to make them the subject of comment is to tacitly condone. Would the Lions have won without serious officiating errors? Who knows? What I am saying is that they, we, should not be in a position where we are left with this question.

51

John Terry should win Champions League with Chelsea before Manchester City move

July 2009

A few seasons ago, with Chelsea flush with the millions Roman Abramovich had pumped into the club, the Matthew Harding Stand taunted Liverpool's Steven Gerrard, telling him he would never play for Chelsea. To rub it in, they followed this by singing, 'We'll buy him anyway.' All that was missing was the waving of bundles of £20 notes.

Gerrard's refusal to join Chelsea, which was closer than some think, was down to loyalty to Liverpool, or, if you are a conspiracy theorist, the result of an orchestrated campaign of abuse towards Gerrard and his family. The anger of Liverpool fans was drowned out with cries about the freedom of choice and the like.

Recent approaches from the new moneybags club, Manchester City, for Chelsea captain John Terry has shown the Stamford Bridge faithful the reality of being on the wrong end of an economic mismatch. It isn't a pleasant feeling and they don't like it. Nobody should be pleased at a smash-and-grab attempt for a player who came through a club's ranks and climbed to the rarefied heights of leading his country; but doesn't it say do unto others?

In a sane world the signing of a five-year contract, which

includes the ludicrous stipulation that a player will remain the club's highest earner even in times of injury and poor form, should be a reliable indication of a player's long-term plans. Clubs should be safe in the knowledge that a player who is a multimillionaire and makes a decision will not have his head turned by money alone. When that player says his commitment has been shown by signing such a document, we should be able to take him at face value.

Two strands of thought emerge from those Chelsea fans who believe Terry can do no wrong and will stay. The first is that this is another episode of Terry renegotiating his contract. If it is, it is becoming increasingly tedious. Having signed a magnificently rewarding contract only recently, it is distasteful for this to be in play again. At some point a club has to say enough is enough, whoever the player. If, as others claim, this is just Terry seeking reassurances over the direction of the club, there are a number of points raised by this. It is a dangerous precedent to allow any player to be the judge of whether a club is or is not planning properly.

He is unlikely to be privy to the right information to make such a call and it is facile to argue that players know which other players are the most talented. That is an entirely different issue. Unless Terry has his own short-, medium- and long-term strategy, one that accounts for the multiple competitions, player fitness and form and so on, he is above himself in believing he knows best.

A final aside on this point; given that Terry would be thirty-four at the end of his contract, there is more than a slim possibility that, with his injury record and fantastically committed style of play, the time will come when a manager should consider whether playing Terry or a younger player is the best choice. This is unavoidable, but how much faith would you have in any player being sufficiently objective to step aside for a player who shows promise but no medals?

Accepting, for argument's sake, that clubs should allow a player this largesse, Terry's method of seeking reassurance is hardly the right way. As captain of the club and a player expressly lauded by his incoming manager, Terry, if he has genuine concerns, should air them in private. He can be as forceful behind closed doors as he wishes, but to create uncertainty and risk alienating supporters is hardly in the club's best interests. If this really is Terry's motivation, why could he not tell Chelsea that unless he heard the right things he would then talk to City? To do this while asking for assurances is to put a gun to the head of his employers, who will now have to slap him down or swallow the public embarrassment of having it known that Terry has ultimate control over their club. Whatever explanations are offered, this is a simple test of loyalty, similar to the one that faced Frank Lampard about a year ago.

Another player who brought success to Chelsea, and without Abramovich's cash, was Gianluca Vialli. Terry could do no better than consider the interview he gave to Radio 5 Live recently, when Vialli set out the issue in a quiet and dignified way, showing common sense, and that he had considered the point from the correct perspective. 'I ask myself, when I finish playing does it matter whether I have in the bank £50 million or £61 million?' the Italian said. If the answer to the above is affirmative then that shows a warped set of values and not one of a true competitor.

You may argue that, in moving to City, Terry would be proving the reverse because he is taking on a challenge to thrust City into the top echelons of English and European football. This would hold water had Terry delivered to his adoring Chelsea faithful everything they sought, but he has not. It is not fair to lay at Terry's feet Chelsea's failure to beat Manchester United in the 2008 Champions League final. Had Didier Drogba demonstrated possession of a brain or Nicolas Anelka shown courage, Terry would not have had to take the penalty in the first place.

Terry owes Chelsea that trophy before he can say his work is done and that he needs a new challenge. Deliver that holy grail and no Chelsea fan would have cause for complaint. Go now and it can only be about cash; no, sorry, even more cash, and that is not the player that Chelsea fans love.

52

'Bloodgate'

July 2009

Background

I was a co-commentator for Radio 5 Live on the Heineken Cup semi-final in which Leinster beat Harlequins 6–5. When Quins fly-half Nick Evans returned to the field after already being substituted and because of an alleged blood injury to Tom Williams, also a replacement, I said, 'Well, at best that is games-manship, and at worst downright cheating.' What transpired was labelled 'Bloodgate', an extraordinary tale of intrigue from which nobody emerges well.

Under the laws of the competition, a player who had already been substituted could not return to the field unless he was replacing a player who had to leave because of a blood injury; if a player was injured in another way, however serious, a substituted player could not return. It was widely known that for some time teams had been finding ways to get round this stipulation by reopening cuts, the use of already bloodied towels and the like; the big difference here was that Dean Richards, Harlequins' Director of Rugby, got caught.

A timeline is set out below to give the reader an idea of how the saga developed. Note the delay in bringing the initial hearing, and then the truncated manner in which the complex appeals were held. Note also that, despite all the appeal hearings taking place on the same day, the independent European Rugby Cup (ERC) disciplinary panel chose to release only the Williams transcript on 25 August, waiting until 2 September to release the remaining evidence; they have repeatedly refused to explain this publicly.

The regulation which Richards was trying to circumvent was introduced in rugby in the early 1990s as a response to the then perceived threat of HIV being passed from player to player as a result of cuts; in fact we now know the virus is not transmittable in the way originally thought, so, ironically, the measure is completely unnecessary.

Timeline of 2009 Events

12 April   – Leinster beat Quins to go through to Heineken Cup final (which they won).

17 April   – ERC officially launch investigation and appoint disciplinary officer Roger O'Connor to gather statements from match officials and players of both teams in addition to reviewing video footage of the game.

20 July   – Williams handed original twelve-month ban at ERC hearing. Dean Richards, Harlequins' club doctor Wendy Chapman and team physiotherapist Steph Brennan cleared of any wrongdoing. Harlequins fined €250,000, half of which is suspended.

7 August   – hours before his right of appeal was due to expire, Williams's lawyers deliver twelve-point demand to his club in return for which he would agree 'to sacrifice' (his words) his appeal against his ban.

8 August   – Dean Richards quits his role as director of rugby at Harlequins.

17 August   – appeal hearings – all heard on the same day before the ERC tribunal in Glasgow:
             – Williams appealed against his ban

- ERC's prosecuting officer appealed against the acquittals of Richards, Brennan and Dr Chapman and the fine against the club (Harlequins ultimately did not resist the appeal).

In reality, the appeal against the acquittals of the three club officials covered different ground from that covered by the first tribunal and should have been the subject of fresh charges; by forcing them to be dealt with as an appeal, the ERC disciplinary committee denied the individuals a right of appeal against what were effectively new charges based on different evidence.

Dean Richards handed three-year ban; Williams's ban reduced to four months; former club physio Steph Brennan, now with England, banned for two years. Dr Chapman was cleared and ERC admitted it did not have jurisdiction to hear her case. Harlequins' fine increased to €300,000, payable in full.

18 August — RFU launch investigation into suggestions of Richards's and Brennan's involvement in four further cases of fake injury (no further action taken). Harlequins told they will not be expelled from Heineken Cup.

25 August — ERC releases transcript solely relating to Williams's appeal; that evidence contained only parts of the evidence available; those parts being prejudicial to the other defendant's.

2 September — ERC releases the remaining appeal transcripts which contained evidence not included in the previously released transcript which included evidence prejudicial to Williams.

Tom Williams made the fall guy at Harlequins in misguided ERC crackdown

23 July 2009

'Hard cases make bad law' is a legal maxim often misused by the common man, but it is entirely apposite to describe the recent rulings made by the independent European Rugby Cup disciplinary panel.

The controversial replacement of Harlequins substitute Tom Williams, for a blood injury, allowed the injured Nick Evans to retake the field and attempt a game-winning dropped goal that would have beaten Leinster in the semi-finals of last season's Heineken Cup.

The precise machinations and culpability of the parties allegedly involved in the incident will be obtained only by the administration of a truth serum, which was beyond even the far-reaching powers of the ERC disciplinary body. They will certainly have made little impact on the Harlequins coach, Dean Richards, with his many years of experience of being cross-examined by Queen's Counsels while he was an officer in the Leicestershire Constabulary.

No doubt Richards expected the decision to go the same way as previous cases, in which there was a suspicion that he or his colleagues had not played by the book: 'Not guilty – we suspect you did it but we cannot find the proof.' He cannot, in his most extreme dreams, have thought they would return a verdict that said: 'Not guilty – we suspect you did it but as we can't prove it we're going to be extra-specially severe on the only person we can decisively put in the frame.'

The transcript of the ERC ruling will make fascinating reading, as it will show how that body was able to be so confident about circumstantial evidence in returning the verdicts. It will also, no doubt, explain what justification there was for finding the player acted on his own in trying to pretend he had been injured.

It should make epic reading, because it surely must address how and why Williams acted in the way alleged. Williams was only on the substitutes' bench for the game and had sat there for the first seventy minutes of the match. If he acted alone, he probably had secreted about him a device to deliver the blood substance to his mouth.

Given that he did not leave the technical area during the second half and was given little notice of the fact that he was replacing another substitute, Chris Malone, he must have had any such device about his person for at least the thirty minutes after half-time. He must also have obtained the said device and brought it to the ground, unless he used the break to nip off to the nearest blood substance-administering device shop.

Given that he was on the field for only five minutes, as a junior player Williams must be remarkably mature and cynical to con-clude independently that, after this short time, the greater good meant that his team needed him to go off and be replaced by an already injured player, who may, or may not, have been able to stand up long enough to take a drop at goal, and in circumstances which were not guaranteed to occur.

Williams did not admit the charge and the finding that cleared the medical staff and Richards necessarily implies that the people who examined the injury were satisfied it was genuine. In the light of all this the ERC must have had other evidence to prove the aforesaid were conned by Williams, that being the inescapable conclusion from their findings.

Despite the claim made by Leinster, their medical staff did not have the right to examine Williams, as the tournament was played under International Rugby Board law, and law 3.10 does not give this right; therefore this does not imply guilt as asserted by Leinster. The fact that Williams was seen to be fiddling with his mouth is not conclusive evidence. The cocky and dull wink given by Williams does not look good, but that alone is insufficient to overcome the difficulties as set out above and prevent the player from plying his trade for a whole year.

It is curious that the club have been fined when their two medical staff and coach were cleared of wrongdoing. If clubs are to be punished for the unilateral actions of their employees, they had better disclose this to their indemnity insurers. Further curiousness is aroused by the size of the club fine, at €250,000 (£216,000). If the club officials were not involved, there is no logical basis for any fine and even if there was a technical reason it should only have been a token. Further, for what reason is half the fine suspended? Suspensions are used to ensure that in the future there is no similar behaviour. If there is no specified behaviour, there can be no repeat and thus no reason for the suspension.

See what I mean about hard cases and bad law?

Of all this, Jeremy Paxman at his magnificently sneering best might say, 'Come off it!' I have no more proof than ERC had, but I think that this was one of an increasing number of occasions when a variety of teams, both club and international, have bent the rules. I applaud the determination of ERC, but they are wrong here.

Quins did not win that game and ERC should have waited for a better case to make their point. Indeed, it would have been better to make no findings in this case but issue a strong message that, should sufficient evidence be available in similar cases, their punishments would be severe.

As it is, they have two parties who for different reasons have got legitimate cause to complain about their punishment, especially Williams, the fall guy. Although we may think in a 'Glenn Hoddle karma' way that they got what was deserved, this is a seriously flawed judgement. The only solution is for substitutes to come and go without restriction; something else that rugby league has got right.

Harlequins' 'Bloodgate' covers nobody in glory

10 August 2009

When commentating for the BBC's Radio 5 Live, I predicted that 'we will hear more about this', referring to the distinctly fishy circumstances surrounding the blood-bin substitution of Harlequins wing Tom Williams, which allowed fly-half Nick Evans to return to the field against Leinster in the Heineken Cup quarter-final. I do not think I could have predicted just how much more was to come.

The 'Bloodgate' affair is one from which not one of the people or bodies concerned can draw any comfort. By dint of their acts, omissions and decisions they have added to rugby's increasing litany of the unacceptable.

That similar undesirables exist in other sports is irrelevant and, while they do not signal rugby's demise, they conclusively mark the death of its hitherto deserved reputation as a sport with superior values. It is true that rugby does not suffer from some of the excesses of football but, unless some line is drawn, they too will be unwelcome visitors on its pitches.

Having been unable to convict and having dismissed charges against any of the Quins officials, the ERC panel handed out a twelve-month playing ban to the only body they could and did convict – Williams. The length of the sentence was clearly excessive in light of the eight-week bans given for the serious offence of gouging.

The decision to absolve all of the Quins officials charged and then fine the club was wrong in principle. If the ERC had not the evidence or courage to convict any Quins official, they had to swallow, however unpalatable it was, their belief that the club had been intimately involved in cheating.

It is claimed by some that the excessive sentence given to Williams was acceptable because it flushed out the true miscreants from the Quins management. To some, the resignation of Dean Richards, the club's director of rugby at the time of the incident, will be justification for the way in which the ERC panel has conducted itself; they are wrong. Getting there in the end is not acceptable when it comes to judicial bodies and where such serious matters are concerned.

Any sentence must relate to only the individual, even if it is meant as a deterrent. It should not be used to discipline indirectly or provoke further action from another party, especially where the very same tribunal has cleared that other of wrongdoing.

You can excuse the use of such ruses when a parent is trying to find out which child set fire to the family dog; artifice has no place in formal disciplinary proceedings, where standards of evidence and justice must be no lower than elsewhere.

With regards to the club, once Quins decided to support Williams's appeal and accept their own erroneous punishment, the subsequent events were set. Accepting a substantial fine clearly signalled acceptance of some guilt.

There is no mechanism or principle whereby a club or country is fined for the sins of an individual, whatever is claimed to the contrary; if this were so, why was the South African Rugby Football Union not fined for Schalk Burger's misdemeanours? Had Quins fought on that point they would have won, because the logical extension of such an intellectually flawed principle would wreak havoc in the future.

Actually, when all is considered, the only thing that the ERC needed to do was punish Williams alone because the same pressure would have faced Quins in any event. In a case where an employee unilaterally cheated and brought the club into disrepute, the correct act for his club would be to terminate his contract. Any refusal to do this by Quins could have drawn allegations that they were not doing this because they knew Williams was not alone in his nefariousness.

Of Richards: first of all he had no responsibility to prove his innocence; he was entitled to rely on the accepted notion that all men are innocent until proven guilty. Moreover, he is the only one who has paid for any part he had in this matter by losing his job.

Of Williams: his must have been the most expensive, as well as stupid, wink in history; without it, however intent were the ERC on making someone pay, they would have had insufficient evidence.

I understand but cannot excuse
Dean Richards's acts

19 August 2009

Dean Richards, the former England player and former copper, is now also the former director of rugby at Harlequins. What will never change is his status as one of the best No. 8 forwards ever to play the game. Some pointed to his apparent lack of athleticism and awkwardness, but they could not explain his seeming omnipresence about the pitch or his singular ability to gather ball cleanly from moving scrums and make telling passes. Nobody doubted his astonishing strength and physical bravery as he competed for the ball on the ground while studs whistled past and often into him.

Deano would probably agree that examples of his rough play are not things of pride; however, they need to be judged in their context. When he was admonished for pummelling Welsh prop Mike Griffiths in a set-to in Cardiff in 1992, his action was to defend me when I was getting a pasting from their front row after a scrum incident; against rugby law but loyal and, some would say in that context, justified.

Presently he is showing one side of his character, by keeping his own counsel about the Bloodgate affair at Harlequins, from which he was the first, and at present only, person to lose his job.

When we played together for England our conversations were wide-ranging but as I was a lawyer and he a policeman, inevitably many times we discussed the law in specific cases and generally. I derided his sense of rough justice, an eye for an eye and all that. All very well, he would say, theoretically; practically things were a good deal vaguer; sometimes things had to be done for the right ending. I now accept he had a point, but there are still some things that should not be excused by the outcome.

Deano loyally served his time in the police and at Leicester rugby club, but I cannot but think that his now apparently dichotomous behaviour has its roots in the loyalty demanded in such institutions. Though such is essential and aspects of it are noble, excessive loyalty to a cause or a group can lead to obfuscation. A non-specific example of this is the alteration of notebook entries – this supports a colleague, but is not sincere.

Deano knows directly what I 'know' only by hearsay – that faking of blood injuries has taken place for a number of years. The imperatives of winning in the professional era and the fact that other teams have acted in similar ways are further pressures that may have led him to stay loyal to his comrades; to win at all costs.

I find it difficult to condemn utterly because I know that my nature, added to the knowledge that my opponents were doing whatever I contemplated, would probably lead me to take the same action and same risk.

I am certain that during the hundreds of interviews and thousands of hours they spanned, PC Richards more than a few times made the point: whatever you say, the fact is that you've been caught.

I cannot excuse what Deano did and although harsh, his punishment is deserved; if you can't do the time . . . I can understand it, however, and he remains my friend. I do not wish to walk away from him.

'Bloodgate': Dean Richards:
I'm sorry I got caught. But I realise
what I did was wrong

22 August 2009

I admit it was not the most subtle way to greet my one-time England colleague Dean Richards as he loomed large at my front door. 'So, how is the man solely responsible for inventing cheating and bringing rugby to its knees?'

As I braced myself for a sharp right-hander, Richards instead looked rueful, even managing the trace of a grin. He half-heartedly joked that he seemed to have had more coverage than Abdelbaset Ali Mohmed al-Megrahi, the released Lockerbie bomber.

Over the past week, rugby has been forced to deal with a storm of criticism over cheating. The fake blood injury acted out by Harlequins wing Tom Williams in the quarter-final of last season's Heineken Cup has forced my sport into a bout of serious soul-searching and led to a three-year ban for Richards, a four-month ban for Williams and a two-year ban for the then Quins physiotherapist, Steph Brennan. Richards, who admitted ordering the substitution to be made, has also resigned from his post as director of rugby at Harlequins. It has been a high price to pay.

We met on Friday at the end of one of the longest weeks of his career. He was full of remorse for the events which have unfolded and, while it does not make what happened right, he deserves credit for his determination to come clean now about what happened in the affair which has become known as 'Bloodgate'.

I started by asking how commonplace faking blood injuries was in top-level rugby.

Dean Richards: I was approached by a few players who had experienced it at other clubs and had experienced cutting. I was not prepared to go down that line. The blood substitution does give you an opportunity to get people off because it doesn't state how much blood and you have the right to take somebody off. This was three or four years ago and they were overseas players. That's how we ended up with blood capsules.

Brian Moore: What made you consider this as an option?

DR: It was quite prevalent and the players felt other teams were having a material advantage by using it and they felt we were missing out.

BM: People will say that just because other people were doing it doesn't mean you have to do it.

DR: And they are right. I've done something wrong and I've got to pay the price for it. At the time, you have the mistaken belief that you are doing the right thing for the club and the players to win the game. I'm also a very competitive person. On this occasion, I asked the physio whether he had some and, when Chris Malone came off [injured], I said I need to use blood. The decision was not made at that point, it was made two or three minutes after Tom Williams had gone on when, in my eyes, he wasn't doing enough to enable us to win the game.

BM: The impression that people have got is that this must have been a management decision.

DR: The allegation from European Rugby Cup was that we would bring Nick Evans off, give him a rest and get him back on, which didn't happen. It was a spur of the moment thing. I asked the physio if there was any blood in the backline to do it legitimately, but there wasn't and time was running out and I said, 'Get Tom off with blood.'

It wasn't done particularly well. When Tom came off, he wiped blood all over his face and he winked at Evans and was staggering around. Even at the time I thought there's obviously something going to be said about this at a later date. Tom went off the pitch and down the tunnel – I didn't speak to him – and he went into the physio room. From there on in, I can't give any direct evidence; the best thing is to ask Tom, the only person who really knows. The first time I saw him after the game is when I addressed the players about ten minutes after the game.

BM: What were you doing from the time he went off to when you addressed the players?

DR: I would have done a television interview. I was also in the tunnel consoling the players as they came in, the other coaches were there and they were upset we had lost the game. That ten minutes seems a long time but it flies by and then after this you address the players. What you tend to find is that the bigger the game the more commitments you have. I had other TV interviews and a press conference. It took me an hour to come back to the changing rooms. I had a shower, changed and went home.

BM: If this was such a big thing, how could you possibly not investigate it fully?

DR: You have to get this into perspective. You are coming into the end of a massive season and we were still in the Guinness Premiership. Although you think there may be an inquiry because of the way Tom came off, until you know, you park it to one side and concentrate on doing your reviews. It was when we were at Sale on the Friday that we found ERC wanted to do an inquiry. I sat down with Tom the following Monday at the training ground – we didn't discuss it before that. It was at this time he told me that, at his direction, he had his lip cut, at his insistence. You then have to make a decision as to which way to go.

BM: You must have known that what you were about to do was wrong?

DR: Without a doubt, but at the time you think you're doing the right thing. About the people around you there's a sense of loyalty; you're trying to safeguard their position: it was the wrong decision made for the right reasons. Had I known then what I know now, I would have fully disclosed. Before we met our lawyers, Tom asked if we should tell them and I said it would put them in a difficult position, so we went into the meeting and nothing was disclosed to the lawyers. We met before he gave evidence on the Friday and, as he left he said, 'There's something I have to tell you, it was me, I did it all.' After he left I was totally bemused and sat for about fifteen minutes thinking how have we got to this stage but I had to dismiss it.

BM: What would you have done if you had been told this before?

DR: We'd have gone in and held our hands up and said we had done something foolish but, because of the position of the people involved, we decided we wanted to go down that route.

BM: What happened after the verdict?

DR: I was shocked. I went to [Harlequins chief executive] Mark Evans the following day [Tuesday 21 July] and said I felt like offering my resignation but Mark said to wait for the written judgement – it drifted on and it became too much and on 3 August, I told Mark I was resigning and it was accepted that week. From Tuesday, I was pushed to one side and the club dealt with things.

The difficulty is this: I still don't know what went on in that room and, had it been one thing and not the other, we could have gone in a different direction.

I did cheat, I knew it was wrong but I thought it was an accepted practice in rugby. I should have been stronger and not have done it. Hopefully, there will be a better system for dealing with this. I am not condoning things but look at Mike Atherton taking something on to the pitch to change the face of the ball and he got a slap on the wrist. Is there any difference? To a point, the people who say that I have damaged the game are right, but it is ironic that the reason we went down the route in the first place was that I didn't want to cut people.

BM: Whenever people say sorry for this, sorry for that, people look at it and say, 'No, you're not, you are sorry you got caught.'

DR: I suppose there is an element of that but hindsight is a wonderful thing. I am sorry I got caught but at the same time I know now, as I did at the time I resigned, that I did the wrong thing.

There you have it. As he left, my guts churned because I knew that, for all his Herculean commitment to English rugby, as a player and a coach, Richards would always be spoken of with this affair mentioned before anything else.

I do not think this matter is closed. The role of the PRA, the ERC and all their advisers needs scrutiny to see what political manoeuvring went on and what was behind Williams's decision to change his evidence. Richards has finally accepted his part in this, and although he should have no credit for that and deserves his punishment, other people in the saga have not been brave enough to do this.

Harlequins success produced by team spirit, not climate of fear

27 August 2009

Tom Williams, the Harlequins wing, effectively pleaded that he was 'only following orders' when he used a fake blood capsule given to him by the club's then physiotherapist, Steph Brennan, at the behest of former director of rugby Dean Richards, to feign injury and be replaced by the previously substituted Nick Evans.

Williams's revised evidence in support of his appeal against a twelve-month ban has now been released by European Rugby Cup. They must have their own reasons for not also releasing the other evidence, because they must know that by doing so they allow us to see only one side. We are therefore more inclined to condemn those whose evidence has been withheld.

Williams's defence was founded on what has been alleged to be a 'climate of fear' created by Richards – one that was so intense that Williams, and presumably all his team-mates, became incapable of independent thought and action.

Accepting that this was an employer/employee relationship, the matters surrounding Williams's action nevertheless have to be considered in the light of the fact that they took place against the background of a team sport, in this case rugby, though the same issues arise with other sports.

The success of a team depends on many factors, but a crucial part of any success is the spirit, or atmosphere, call it what you will, that exists within and around the team. Occasionally this is not dictated by the manager or coach – the successful England rugby sides captained by Will Carling and Martin Johnson largely created the required environment for themselves. Far more often, particularly in football, the input of the manager is the dominant factor.

There are many ways to create the necessary ambience and there are innumerable anecdotes about how managers and coaches, from a variety of eras, were able to fashion the right tone for their clubs. There are common themes with winning teams, especially ones that are successful over an extended period.

Respect and trust between players and managers are things which are earned in sport and their absence almost certainly guarantees failure for a team. Those two things are never achieved solely by creating a climate of fear. Even a manager as successful as football's Sir Alex Ferguson, who is eminently capable of giving stick when it is required, counterbalances his approach. Though Ferguson's empathetic side is not often revealed, a succession of his players at Manchester United will attest to its existence.

Harlequins finished second in last season's Premiership, only four years after being relegated. Fifty per cent of their regular team came from the club's academy and they had fewer international players than many of their rivals. Harlequins' coach John Kingston on Monday attributed last season's achievements to what he described as Quins' greatest asset – their team spirit.

Williams's claim that Richards was not challenged was his main justification for his part in 'Bloodgate'. Williams said of Richards: 'He ran the show. He did not discuss his decisions with me. He gave directions, and these were followed.' Well, yes, he was the manager. But how could Richards have created such a successful team spirit in a climate of fear? Looking back through countless media interviews, some from Williams, there is little evidence of an authoritarian regime, not even in satirical form.

Williams's actions after he faked the injury are explained by his self-proclaimed automatism. He stated: 'I would like to say that I was presented with a huge dilemma when I was handed the blood capsule. However, in reality I was so programmed to Dean's authority and focused on the game that there were no such considerations.'

All of which explains his wink when exiting the field . . .

Williams also claimed that he was told he was on the fringe of the England international set-up. He may find that Martin Johnson may not look positively on any player with a self-confessed inability to think or act independently when under pressure.

By all means condemn the others who have had, or may face, severe punishment, but let us proceed no longer with the image of a beatified Tom Williams.

Disciplinary bodies must act fairly with rugby careers on the line

31 August 2009

The start of the new season cannot come quickly enough for rugby. The past few weeks have seemed a lifetime as 'Bloodgate' has spilled across every media platform and brought opprobrium from all quarters. Sorry: there is a good way to go yet. While the ERC drip-feeds information, for reasons known only to itself, and things happen like last week's resignation of Harlequin chairman Charles Jillings, this festering sore will remain exposed. In his resignation press release Jillings revealed information that added to the concerns about the way ERC and its disciplinary tribunal handled the recent hearings and the way in which it continues to release information on a partial basis.

Immediately the judgements were handed down at the first hearing (Tom Williams banned for twelve months, everyone else cleared but the club fined substantially) worrying flaws were apparent. Many people claimed that those who complained about these flaws were trying to minimise the culpability of those guilty of lying and cheating. However, as the full extent of their seriousness becomes clear, every fair-minded person should be shocked and concerned and there must be an independent investigation into the conduct of ERC and possibly the Professional Rugby Players' Association and Williams's representatives.

Every club and every person within that club should be fully aware that if they ever find themselves subject to the jurisdiction of ERC they will be subject to a system under which they may be subject to double jeopardy.

ERC's prosecutor was allowed to appeal and reopen matters of fact dealt with at the first hearing; moreover, a statement from Williams detailing events occurring after the first hearing was accepted as admissable in evidence. His discussions with his employer were not only confidential, but were post fact and irrelevant to the matters which were being heard.

Dean Richards's legal team received important appeal papers one working day before the appeal hearing, making it practically impossible to deal properly with new claims, and a plea for a reasonable postponement fell on deaf ears.

Williams's claim that a climate of fear existed, which pressured him to cooperate in the fake blood scam, was accepted as fact on the basis of his written testimony alone. No cross-examination was allowed, nor could other parties call witnesses to refute this assertion, on which was founded the claim of duress.

Because ERC released one out of five judgements, only Williams's version of events has been seen and this has allowed allegations to become fact in many quarters. Jillings has been tarred with the slight that he was in charge of an organisation in which bullying was acceptable. The entire management and coaching staff are therefore tainted as being associated with and accepting such a regime. Derek McGrath, ERC's chief executive, recently stated that because four judgements were still to be released, ERC was a party to the system, like everybody else. Jillings's statement supported claims made in the press that members of ERC met with Williams' representatives between the first hearing and its appeal.

McGrath must answer the following: did ERC meet as claimed? Why? When? What was discussed? Was any deal done between the parties?

Given ERC's position, to speak to only one of a number of

defendants, all part of the same legal process, without telling anybody, is wrong. Is McGrath going to investigate these damning
allegations and, if they are true, will he resign, as has Jillings,
because it happened on his watch? What measures would be taken
against any ERC person involved in any secret meeting?

Much has been made of the employer/employee relationship
which, it is claimed, intensified the pressure on Williams to comply
with nefarious orders. However, within that arrangement was
also a duty of fidelity requiring Williams to act at all times in good
faith.

If Jillings is right, Williams was far from the hapless fall guy por-
trayed in some parts. Discussing confidential contractual issues
with a third party would not appear to be good faith. Having
secret meetings, as Jillings alleges, would also not seem to comply
with that duty.

There may still be people who think that in this case two
wrongs do make a right, but governing bodies have an absolute
duty to act properly at all times. Disciplinary bodies, with the
power to end careers, should not exercise their powers in anything
other than a scrupulously fair way. If either deviates from these
duties they are no better than those on whom they pass judgement. Fairness is not a moveable feast according to what outcome
is politically desirable.

You may think such things are insubstantial compared to the
issues of cheating and lying. If you faced career-threatening
charges and such things were allowed, would you still think them
unimportant?

We shouldn't forget that Tom Williams was prepared to lie again

3 September 2009

The bewildering facts and legal issues arising out of the 'Bloodgate' affair were augmented by the release of European Rugby Cup's written judgements against Harlequins and their former director of rugby and physiotherapist, Dean Richards and Steph Brennan, respectively.

The condemnation of the public and majority of the media has been focused on Richards, with the club and Brennan a close second and Tom Williams being seen as the hapless victim; ERC, the governing body, has received little criticism.

Richards has been punished and deservedly so, likewise Brennan, but their guilt does not excuse the actions of other people who have outstanding matters for which they must account, or give a credible explanation.

To point out those faults and ask for them to be dealt with is not to seek to minimise the culpability of the club or its former employees; it is to try to ensure that the full details and roles of all involved see the light of day and that the public jury is not misled.

The publication in *Telegraph* Sport of the eleventh-hour demands made by Williams suggests that once the club's most senior officers discovered the details of what had taken place they tried to deal with the matter correctly.

Careful scrutiny of the demands and Harlequins' response

reveals two seminal phrases from which much flows: 'Tom . . . is prepared to sacrifice his appeal on the following basis', and 'The club cannot make payments to your client that are conditional on him not exercising his legal rights'.

When you read those statements, which party is trying to influence the actions of the other? Even as late as six hours before his time to appeal expired, Williams was still prepared to stick with his lies at the original disciplinary hearing, for a price. What should now be clear is that if Harlequins had really wanted to continue with the cover-up, all they had needed to do was meet Williams's demands.

ERC's prosecutor had not appealed Williams's sentence, only those against the club, Richards and Brennan and the decision not to proceed with the case against the club doctor.

While he could have argued that the fine for the club was too low, he would not have had any other evidence with which to try to reopen the cases against the individuals; as such his appeals either would not have been heard or they would have been bound to fail, because the panel could not have reached a different verdict having not convicted previously on the same facts.

Harlequins would have suffered less by accepting Williams's offer and ERC and its disciplinary officer would have been left fuming but with no alternative remedies. If the senior figures had acted improperly, as alleged, they would have taken this route; that they chose not to bow to Williams's demands and to face all the opprobrium that has flowed from that decision is not indicative of guilt.

In addition, you will notice that it is claimed in Williams's demand that, on the advice of the Professional Rugby Players' Association, it would only be worth appealing if the player could be reasonably confident of getting his ban reduced to three months; or presumably thereabouts.

This leads us back to the disclosed meetings which former chairman Charles Jillings claimed in his resignation statement last week took place between Williams and representatives of ERC before this demand was made.

ERC has so far refused to answer questions posed by this column concerning those meetings; it should now do so. And I add a further question: was there any inducement offered to Williams?

The lateness of Williams's demand, coming six hours before his deadline to file an appeal expired, also highlights the fact that virtually no time was given to the other legal teams properly to prepare their cases.

Even though the lawyers indicated they were happy to go ahead, privately they have said that this was only because they did not want to risk the further wrath of the panel when they were only arguing mitigation.

Of ERC itself, could a governing body have done more damage to rugby by its handling of this whole matter if it had tried? You may say that it got to the truth, but the details above show that it managed to do so only because Harlequins did not accede to Williams's demands and governing bodies should not act in this way anyway.

The most serious question, among many others, for ERC to answer is this: why was the Williams judgement released before the others, and why in the earlier judgement was the evidence of Williams's demands and the refusals by Harlequins not in the body of the judgement?

If it is said they were not relevant, on what basis was this extraordinary conclusion based? Why are full details of the other parties' accounts not available, as opposed to precis of certain dissenting comments?

ERC should also explain the haste with which the witnesses, respondents and their advisers were obliged to appear and deal with matters at the appeal, which contrasts starkly with the delay in presenting the judgements to the public. What was the hurry?

There is the world of difference between giving somebody the right to present their case and allowing that to be done fully. This governing body's practice should be judged against those of the Rugby Football Union, led by their disciplinary officer Jeff Blackett, when handling the recent case involving Bath.

Had Williams not appealed the doctor would not have been placed in the spotlight. Whether she has to face her own professional body depends on the testimony of Williams, who despite having his ban reduced was still found by the ERC to have been a liar and cheat.

The combination of selective inclusion of testimony and evidence and the timing of its release has allowed inaccurate assumptions to be made. This should not have happened with a competent body.

I believe the full truth has still not come out.

ERC should come clean over Harlequins scandal

10 September 2009

I am a former captain of Harlequins. I am also a friend of Dean Richards. He lied and cheated, his punishment was harsh but deserved. Quins were rightly punished and had they been banned from this season's Heineken Cup they could not have complained.

I make the above statement because I have had an agenda over the 'Bloodgate' affair: I want justice to be done properly, all the facts and actions of all the parties to be known and all outstanding questions to be answered.

If this means that the Rugby Football Union inquiry under Judge Jeff Blackett finds evidence to support charges that could not have been brought by European Rugby Cup, then so be it. If Mark Evans, the Harlequins chief executive, is proven guilty under such a charge he would have to resign or be dismissed.

However, in assisting Blackett's inquiry it is interesting that ERC stated after their last meeting that they had authorised only relevant evidence to be passed, when appropriate, to Blackett. Given ERC's refusal to answer serious questions about its part in this affair and the way its disciplinary panel allowed judgements to be released on different dates and to contain selective and damaging material, I and many others had doubts about this being done properly.

I wrote to the RFU seeking reassurance that it would demand

ERC handed over all evidence because of the above concerns; also making the point that a third party could not decide for Blackett what he (Blackett) deemed relevant to his own inquiry. Unlike with ERC, I swiftly received a reply confirming that the RFU will be demanding that ERC hands over all evidence, including statements. Contrast the two organisations' openness about the process and willingness and speed in answering questions.

The refusal by ERC to come clean is made worse by the fact that it discussed some of the questions I raised on 25 August. When asked why the Williams judgement was released eight days before the remaining judgements, Professor Lorne Crerar, the chairman of the panel, said that this was done because the Williams matter was heard first.

Notwithstanding the fact that all the appeals were heard on the same day, that answer is also flatly contradicted by the contents of his own judgement in the Richards case and other cases. Crerar knows that the first dealings before the appeal panel were with the jurisdictional arguments in the cases of Richards and the former Harlequins physiotherapist, Steph Brennan.

Not only is the ERC not dealing straight with the public, it is dealing with its own members in the same way. The question therefore remains: what was the real reason for the separate release of the judgements?

I think new questions should now be answered, such as why is that reason being withheld? Did either the ERC disciplinary officer, Roger O'Connor, or his solicitor, Max Duthie, have any discussions with the panel about the judgements and their release? If so, what was said? What persuaded the panel to take a step so unusual; one for which none of the thirteen senior advocates, sports administrators and disciplinary officers from three sports I asked to consider this matter could find a legitimate reason?

When pressed further about whether the panel's handling of the cases had harmed rugby's image, Crerar then retreated behind the age-old excuse that he had a day-time job and other pressures to deal with. Precisely my point: a bunch of amateurs meddling in the world of professional rugby, reserving and exercising powers with which they are not fit to deal.

The ERC chief executive, Derek McGrath, continues to avoid answering questions and should his organisation be found to have damaged rugby will he, like Quins' former chairman, Charles Jillings, resign?

In the early days of professionalism, I was the first chairman of the Professional Rugby Players' Association.

Damian Hopley almost single-handedly created that important organisation, but his role in this also needs explanation. His involvement should not have gone beyond organising separate representation for Harlequins wing Tom Williams, his member. It is now clear that he became personally involved in the case, attending meetings and speaking to the press, and he should give an account of exactly what he did and when.

It would be particularly interesting to know if he was aware of his member's eleventh-hour, twelve-point offer put to Quins in return for sacrificing his appeal. If he did not know, what did he think of his member's proposal; one that would, had it been met, prevented ERC from getting the evidence which had to form the basis of any negotiations on a sentence reduction.

No doubt there will be a rash of stories and further leaks to try to deflect us from asking these questions. I appear to be one of the few interested in asking for all parties to account for what they did.

However, there is a growing body of opinion, among both supporters and chief executives of clubs over which ERC has jurisdiction, that wants answers and will not be fobbed off with further silence and spin.

Whatever their reasons or motives, Williams, Richards, Brennan and Jillings have all eventually fronted up – are the people and organisations questioned above big enough to do likewise?

Postscript

Are the ERC and IRB the new Fédération Internationale de l'Automobile?

31 May 2010

I told you so.

I usually have little time for those who revel in *Schadenfreude*, but this time I am enjoying the public discomfort felt by the officials from European Rugby Cup Ltd and the International Rugby Board over their inability to draft and impose a uniformly binding ban on Dean Richards for his part in the 'Bloodgate' affair.

I would not be feeling a good measure of joy about this had it not been for the disgraceful way ERC ignored repeated and legitimate questions about serious deficiencies in their prosecution of Richards et al., refusing to front up while hoping it would all go away. It would be different had the IRB, situated in the same Dublin office block as the ERC, not simply rubber-stamped the whole thing and refused to investigate such serious concerns.

At the time I covered 'Bloodgate' I was accused of being all manner of things. I was an apologist for Richards, even though those alleging this could not specify a single word of mine which excused his behaviour or contested the length of his sentence.

My desire that the governing body for Europe's premier club tournament should ensure its disciplinary process was subject to best practice and be fair in both letter and spirit drew allegations of pedantry and myopia. What do technicalities and minutiae matter? They got there in the end.

Well, what has transpired shows why seemingly small and inconvenient things like competence, fairness and process, even when dealing with wrongdoers, matter a great deal. If ERC had spent more time getting their practices in order and concentrated on drafting and imposing an unambiguous and binding ban, instead of rushing out one judgement out of five to influence public opinion in their favour; if they had not allowed their agents to brief the press regularly; if they had had the balls to answer uncomfortable questions – then we would not be where we are, with rugby getting another kicking in the court of media and public opinion.

There is a delicious irony in the embarrassed splutterings of the ERC and IRB. Having previously no regard for the spirit of their disciplinary process, releasing evidence, for example, to defendants with only one working day to prepare submissions, they now claim that whatever the legal niceties, what is being done is not within the spirit of the sentence. Leaving aside that sentences do not have a spirit, how can you expect a defendant who is treated without regard to the spirit of due process to abide by it? I think the ban should have been all-encompassing but it is not Richards's fault, nor mine, nor the RFU's that it is not. It is the fault of those I criticised at the time of the scandal and those now shown to be the serial incompetents I said they were when nobody wanted to listen.

You have to smile at the attempts to bash the RFU's disciplinary supremo Judge Jeff Blackett over his ruling on the wording of the ban. Some observers even fail to understand that he did not draft it, and when he was asked to rule had to do so without regard for trying to save the faces of ERC and the IRB. They stand aghast at Blackett's refusal to compromise his professional integrity in favour of some sort of fraternity within rugby.

You see, this is what happens when things like this go before proper lawyers; it is what would have happened if this had been taken to the High Court. When justice is not done properly in every respect and it comes up against real courts, real laws and real lawyers, a sport's governing body, as the FIA found out in the Briatore case, is not able simply to shift things around for its political convenience. It is not allowed to say, 'Oh well, we wrote this, but really we meant that, and why can't we just alter the clause to cover our mistake?' It cannot fall back on what it claims is the spirit of its actions.

And what now of ERC chief executive Derek McGrath and disciplinary officer Roger O'Connor? The former is in overall charge of ERC and the latter had direct charge of this whole unsatisfactory farce, one which has brought rugby into disrepute in so many ways.

Charles Jillings, the former Harlequins chairman, did nothing wrong, despite the unsubstantiated allegations widely thrown at him. Even so, he resigned because he said it happened on his watch. This act in today's times was said to evidence his guilt when in fact it was evidence of honour and an acceptance of responsibility. Will McGrath and O'Connor be similarly honourable and accept responsibility or will they blame everyone else and hide in a corner like last time?

53

Keep Ashes sledging witty not personal

August 2009

Giles Clarke, the chairman of the England and Wales Cricket Board, feels it necessary to issue an edict in the programme for the fourth Test between England and Australia at Headingley. In it he demands an end to boorish behaviour and comment against Ricky Ponting, the Australian captain and batsman supreme. Why he felt compelled to do this, God only knows. Leave aside all the arguments that the Aussies give more than they get, that they invented sledging, as well as whingeing and the like.

Ponting does not want or need any patronising interference on his behalf. Like all true sporting icons, he has repeatedly shown that abusive comments or gestures are mere trifles which he can either ignore or use as inspiration, making any subsequent success all the more satisfying.

David 'Bumble' Lloyd, the effusive Sky commentator and lover of jousting, recently averred that the dividing line between the acceptable and unacceptable depended on whether the remarks were 'personal'. He did not go on to clarify his interpretation of this touchstone and thus he leaves us free to decide what we consider indelicate. This presents us with a problem: which of several definitions of 'personal' do we prefer?

It is unwise to presuppose anything that goes on in Bumble's head, but he, like all normal people, civilised people, will accept that there are boundaries which should not be crossed, but also that it is hellishly difficult to be precise about what they are. Most likely they are phrases that fit dictionary definitions: relating to somebody's private life, referring offensively to somebody or unfairly remarking about or questioning others.

Only the dull or the drunk would think that remarks about a player's children are suitable, and it is tempting to include a player's wider family in the list of the prohibited.

However, there are other meanings: relating to one person, done by one person only and intended for somebody. A player's idiosyncrasies may be used to mock and, though 'personal', they are not automatically offensive.

Being a ready wit himself, Bumble would probably agree that humour compounds the dilemma. To illustrate the extent of the conundrum, do you see any difference, in terms of legitimacy, in the following two examples of comment?

'Your mother is a whore' and 'You should have been a professional, like your mother', or 'Oi, big-nose' and 'Oi, your nose is so big you could smoke a cigar in the showers'. They mean the same; the difference is that in each case the latter is, to most of us, funny.

Although you may not find them hugely amusing, you must at least concede that there is an attempt to entertain within the insults. The former demonstrate hardly any thought at all, and so it is with booing. If Clarke had limited himself to decrying this childish species of insult and any instances of straight abuse, there would be little with which to argue. But terms like 'respect' are so subjective that they give only loose guidance.

Sky has taken an editorial decision to fade out most of the comments made between the English and Aussie cricketers. That is justifiable, it might even be contractual, but it is unfortunate as viewers are tempted to denounce all exchanges as mere squabbling. If we could hear what was said, for example between Stuart Broad and Mitchell Johnson at Edgbaston, we could make up our own minds about what was going on and whether we approved.

The International Cricket Council would probably not find

favour with a proposal that the stump microphones should be turned up. Any objection would be right if it were to prevent us sitting through six hours of 'Oooh, nice one Brett/Swanny' from the wicketkeepers, but not if it were to stop the exposure of real examples of vileness.

Knowing that his comments were being heard by hundreds of thousands might be a restraining influence on a player. It could be argued this would encourage players to verbal each other, but it is doubtful that viewers would find constant comment acceptable. Moreover, players would have to take into account that there is no agreed standard of what is amusing when it comes to banter.

The above could be used as an excuse to bring out countless hackneyed, as well as hilarious, cricketing sledges from the past, but one instance from the fifth Test at the Oval in 2001 is worth retelling. England's James Ormond was a relatively unknown figure at the time he took guard. His team were seven wickets down and 328 runs behind a crowing Aussie XI who, incidentally, included one Ricky Ponting.

As Ormond took guard, Mark Waugh tried the following: 'Mate, no way are you good enough to play Test cricket', which is not funny and too subjective to be effective. Ormond's brilliant, impromptu retort was deeply personal. 'Maybe not,' he replied, 'but at least I'm the best player in my family.'

I wish I'd said that, though I did come up with a description of a game against the French rugby team that said it was like playing against fifteen Eric Cantonas – brilliant, but brutal.

54

One FA rule for the 'Big Four' and one for everyone else

September 2009

How can Manchester United not be charged after a fan got on to the pitch and a missile was thrown from the crowd in the weekend's game against Manchester City at Old Trafford? How can Arsenal not have a case to answer for their fans attempting to get on to the pitch and injuring a steward when they played Manchester City?

Apparently, because there was alleged provocation from Emmanuel Adebayor in the latter case and Craig Bellamy unwisely got himself involved with the trespassing fan in the former, the Football Association apparently thinks the clubs do not merit a charge.

First, the proximity of a player has nothing to do with a club's responsibility for the behaviour of their fans and, second, what sort of precedent does all this set?

The incidents at the recent West Ham v. Millwall game do not differ in principle to the above events, only in degree. Therefore, the lawyers for both of those two clubs will be poring over the reasoning for the FA failing to discipline their 'Big Four' colleagues, no doubt to see whether their previous statements that they would not contest charges should be reversed.

Finally, on the incidents in the Manchester derby, when are football's masters going to use a sensible method of time-keeping, like a stop-clock, something used in team sports all over the world and in such disparate games as American football, hockey and lacrosse among others?

No more arguing about whether the amount of time added is correct or whether that time was actually played. No more electronic boards that nobody can see when the sun is out. No more post-match blaming something else, rather than the fact that your team did not concentrate right up to the final whistle.

It is that simple – or is this sermonising?

55

Andy Murray should turn his back on incompetent LTA blazers

September 2009

Last week's valiant struggle by Andy Murray to keep Great Britain in the second division of world tennis failed and when the contributions of Messrs Henman, Rusedski and Murray are taken out of the country's Davis Cup results for the last twenty years, Britain have failed to win a single match.

Anyone involved in sport was aware of the truly awful mismanagement of the Lawn Tennis Association and behind it the All England Club. However, never fear, the LTA had a cunning plan back in 2005 when they submitted a memorandum to the Select Committee on Culture, Media and Sport, saying it aimed to have five or six players in the world top 100 by 2009.

When the LTA's chief executive Roger Draper launched the Blueprint for Tennis in October 2006, he said we want 'many more warriors coming through who can deal with pressure situations' and 'by 2012, we should have five or six players in the top 100'. Two days ago he was quoted as saying, 'Don't judge us on the short term but in five to seven years.' If you don't like the goalposts, just move them.

Neither Tim Henman nor Greg Rusedski were given the credit they deserved for their unfailing support of the GB cause and Murray should not suffer the same fate. However, we are reaching the point where he should put his own career first and nobody ought to blame the Scot if he did. He should go his own way; only then will the true awfulness of the situation become apparent.

He can make his return conditional on the removal of the blazered officials whose stewardship has brought tennis to this low ebb and about whom John Lloyd recently railed. He should also join the few professional people trying to arrest this decline and demand an end to the socially elitist attitude of the sport.

56

Sport's orgy of double standards is irritating and hypocritical

September 2009

It is the holier-than-thou season at the moment. Cheating, lying, fake blood, gouging, drug-taking rugby union has been getting it from cheating, lying, gouging (Chinese), drug-taking, stabbing, rioting, racist-anti-Semitic-homophobic-chanting football.

Never slow to have a dig at its more successful relative, drug-taking (Gareth Hock), lying, cheating (Canterbury Bulldogs), bottom-fingering (John Hopoate) rugby league has got in on the act. Even former internationals of substance-coating, cheating, lying table tennis have sermonised. At least lying, cheating, race-fixing Formula One has had the sense to keep its own counsel.

Rightly aggrieved Leinster fans have pointed at Harlequins but do not think there should be a similarly emotion-led inquiry into their team's apparently dodgy uncontested scrum incident in the previous round of last year's Heineken Cup.

European Rugby Cup and its 'process-challenged' independent disciplinary panel are still hiding from uncomfortable questions on 'Bloodgate' and know that the fallout from unearthing evidence that the Heineken Cup-winning side cheated would be catastrophic – best not go there then.

Some individuals have unwisely joined in this orgy of double standards. Many a smile met Lawrence Dallaglio's utterances on cheating. Leicester Tigers fans used to have a sweepstake on what minute Wasps would pull the old uncontested scrum ploy when they faced them. Moreover, unless Lol is certain his career was taintless, he should work privately on the Rugby Football Union investigative Task Force.

Arsène Wenger's legendary myopia and amnesia concerning his own players' fouls contrasts markedly with his clear view and moral certainty about Emmanuel Adebayor's misbehaviour last weekend. His certainty about the intent behind his former player's acts is curious, given his claim that his own player, Eduardo, could not be guilty because intent to deceive could never be proved.

And wherever you find Wenger, Sir Alex Ferguson cannot be far away. Of Eduardo's alleged dive, the Scot said, 'I wouldn't say it publicly but I wouldn't be pleased if it was my player who did that', but that 'When you make a public criticism of your players you are in danger of losing the morale of the dressing room.' Ferguson's justification for public silence is no excuse and his real priorities are revealed by the words that followed: 'Your job is to protect the dressing room and keep it solid.'

For Sir Alex's words to be seen as anything other than a self-serving, opportunistic attack on a bitter rival, he has to give details of how he censures his players in private when they commit similar acts. His stance exacerbates the problem; until high-profile managers are brave enough to criticise them publicly, players are tacitly encouraged to continue.

Perhaps it would be better that future criticism of sports be made on the narrow basis of what is being discussed, without reference to other sports, unless those sports offer a solution to the problem in hand.

Another area that causes the greatest difficulty for all involved in, or commenting on, sport is when anything arises that has a legal element. Fulsome sermons on the moral correctness of some or other decision collide with the legal process, something that should have no emotion if it is to do a proper job.

Lawyers, although despised, are habitually engaged to advocate

in front of quasi-judicial bodies and they love incidents sur-
rounded by emotion; it opens up all manner of possibilities to
exploit the partiality and muddled thinking that invariably accom-
pany indignation.

Football has rightly been criticised for not using a retrospective
system of video review and citing and when Uefa finally found the
courage to use this potent disciplinary method, most people said
'about time'. Unfortunately, Uefa inadequately managed the exercise from start to finish and difficult consequences arise from
its latest blunder. Uefa should have announced its intentions before
the season started and made clear how it would operate and
the likely range of punishments before suddenly focusing on
Eduardo's 'dive'.

UEFA was at best reactionary and this looked like another in a
series of observations, comments and interfering by the Franco-
German axis that runs football. It might not yet amount to an
anti-English plot, but it does demonstrate an unbalanced interest
in all things to do with English teams.

Above all, for this measure to gain acceptance UEFA should
have ensured the first case brought was unarguable. It is right that
Eduardo's ban was rescinded because the case could not make
out; the fault lies with those prosecuting, whatever the 'morality'
of what happened. UEFA has not been craven, it has been stupid.

It has also given succour to those who oppose this method
because it cannot be totally decisive. It does not need to be effective. If there is ambiguity, some guilty players will go unpunished,
but at the time they dive they have no idea what camera has what
angle of the incident.

The thinking around Adebayor's recent actions is becoming
similarly irrational. Some say he could have provoked a riot and
as a result should get harsher punishment. His sentence should
have no link to the vehemence of the crowd's reaction.

Arsenal fans were at liberty to protest verbally, but once they
chose to confront Adebayor they were responsible solely for their

acts; if this is not so, fans will be incentivised to react in a more extreme manner, knowing that this may increase the offending player's punishment.

Whether people like it or not, the legal process has developed this way for good reasons. If a point is difficult, it is tempting to view it as a technicality, something that is optional when searching for the wider goal of justice. The problem is that your technicality is someone else's fundamental right, and given that there is a presumption of innocence, alleged technicalities should be construed in favour of a defendant.

When you start to cut corners, you open up the possibility of seriously flawed judgements; and worse, if you get a panel that is dishonest – and this does happen – it can defend its judgements because of precedents set by previous panels ignoring or bending rules.

Laws must be well thought out, clear, well-known and consistently exercised.

57

Ukraine v. England on the internet is the future of football viewing

October 2009

History will be created on Saturday when, for the first time, a match involving the England football team will be broadcast exclusively on the internet. I shall be one of those paying to watch through offers on this website.

The reaction caused by this has, at times, bordered on the hysterical and demonstrates the divide that exists between the internet generation and the rest. It also has behind it motives which are, at best, self-interested and these are related to the wider themes of media ownership and, above all, hard cash and lots of it. In the longer term, the whole issue of rights broadcasting is at stake and if you think this fanciful, read on – there are billions of pounds riding on this.

There have been the usual debates about whether all England games should be available free-to-air. There is little merit in the complaints that, along with the subscriptions for Sky, Setanta and now ESPN, football fans have been made to pay through the nose, and the demand for £5 to watch Ukraine v. England, rising to £12, is a step too far. However, this is merely an economic argument. The principle of free-to-air was long ago conceded when the rights holders, including the FA and Premier League, took Sky's money.

The argument that not everyone has access to the internet is similarly bogus. Although 30 per cent of people do not have access to the internet, this is a smaller percentage than those who do not have Sky TV. Moreover, that doesn't seem to be a problem when huge sums of money are on offer to purchase TV rights.

So what are the real reasons for this rumpus? One of the reasons is good old-fashioned technophobia. Indeed, some of the questions raised around the whole subject show how far behind recent technological advances large sections of the public and press remain. Although most people are familiar with e-mail and browsing, some are just not comfortable with the internet as a means of accessing entertainment. This is not helped by the procedure involved in subscribing for the game, which has little to do with security, but much to do with the fact that both the broadcaster and web-management companies know the value of the database created by making would-be buyers register.

A further reason is the fear raised, deliberately or otherwise, about the broadcast experience. This is groundless: provided a viewer has broadband, the experience offered will be of similar quality to any other broadcast medium.

Pubs and clubs which screen sport will not have a problem, provided they have either a plasma screen or the equivalent. As these are essentially monitors, all that needs to be done is for the PC or laptop to be connected by two wires and, hey presto, you have a large viewing screen for the web stream.

There are drawbacks to internet-based broadcasting: anyone with a connection speed below broadband will not be able to view the game, and viewers are limited to watching on whatever sized screen they have available. However, most of the criticism is commercially based and some has probably been deliberately manufactured. The *Sunday Times* and the *Sun* are both offering the game, but appear to have divergent views on whether it is a good idea. This is unusual given News International's well-known policy of protecting its interests in whatever way it can.

Take a look at the revenues generated from a football fan who is new to satellite broadcasting and wants to have the option to watch all Premiership and England games. To access football on Sky, after set-up charges of £79, the Sky basic package plus Sky Sports 1 costs £318 a year and a further £108 if fans want Sky Sports 2. Additionally, access to the remaining forty-six Premiership matches on ESPN is a further £108. Total price: £534 a year. Pubs and clubs that screen Sky TV have to fork out thousands for a commercial licence.

The BBC annual licence fee is £142.50 and this covers TV, radio and online.

Those involved in the internet have long identified this potential threat to traditional broadcasting and the huge riches it provides. For the past ten years, BT have been working towards providing a means to send outside broadcasts down the wire, thus making the huge satellite trucks presently required unnecessary, with the attendant cost savings. If this becomes reality, it is a short leap for a club to fix cameras at its ground and with a good quality software package and a decent director, clubs will become their own broadcasters – if even a minority of Manchester United's rumoured one million fans worldwide stumped up £3 per game, you can see the potential revenues.

Add to that, revenue from cross-selling merchandise online to such a huge database and suddenly there is a very good reason for clubs to go their own way. If that happened, the existing gap between the big and smaller clubs would be even wider.

As for the supporter; when you do the maths, the prospect of reliable quality internet broadcasting at a fiver a pop seems good value. After all, how many fans watch 106 games on TV at home and how many pubs and clubs screen 1,680 games in their premises each season?

Once broadband Britain is a reality, the truly 'available-for-all' policy might be to offer England games only through the internet.

★

Ferguson gets us all to look the other way – again

Sir Alex Ferguson's ability to direct media attention whither he will is second to none. He was at it again after the disappointing 2–2 draw with Sunderland.

If you scan the press you will find relatively little analysis of United's performance, the focus being on Ferguson's comment that the referee, Alan Wiley, was not fit enough to referee at the top level. This is exactly as desired by Ferguson and, although the ruse is transparent, it seems to work every time.

58

We need a shift in attitude towards disability sport

October 2009

Jimmy Carr recently made the following joke: 'Say what you like about servicemen amputees from Iraq and Afghanistan, but we're going to have a fucking good Paralympic team in 2012.'

The VOPs (vicariously offended persons) soon denounced Carr, in contrast to the majority view of troops as expressed on their own websites, such as the Army Rumour Service.

As Carr's comment did not criticise or ridicule the servicemen, the objectors must believe that the subject cannot be the basis of humour and that logically any similarly sensitive subject must also be off-limits.

What should outrage people, and what really offends servicemen, is the real scandal of underequipping and overcommitting of our armed forces; and the fact that members of the public have complained about having to share swimming pools with amputees.

Politicians, keen to avert eyes from their own nefariousness, have also jumped on the bandwagon of outrage. We are now being told what we can and cannot find funny.

Actually, it is legitimate to see a compliment behind the joke – these men have the courage to overcome their handicap and are the sort of people who will strive to represent their country again, albeit in a different arena and one where at least they will know why they are there.

Unfortunately, as with their service careers, they will find that the attitude of some of the public and officialdom is patronising and occasionally hostile, on the basis that their disability is an unwelcome reminder of the real and brutal consequences of war.

Even though not deliberately so, too much coverage of disability sport is similarly condescending, with the focus being on the injury, its origins and effects, as opposed to the usual features of sport like form, fitness and technique. Once the human-interest point has been made, all disabled athletes want or need is for their performances to be assessed and reported in the same way as their able-bodied counterparts. This means criticism when justified, and not some variation of 'but they did well anyway considering all they've been through'.

This is the reason that the title Paralympics is meant to mean the 'Parallel Olympics' rather than 'Paraplegic Olympics'.

We need a shift in attitude towards disability sport. The BBC, with its public service remit, does far more than other broadcasters, but satellite TV provides very little coverage and then it is only tangential to able-bodied sport.

The argument is the same as with women's sport and produces the same difficulty. It is not worth reporting because the standard is too low to be of interest. It will not get to the required standard without reporting to show its availability and to attract sponsorship.

For the time being, even if this is initially a sop, the media has to provide the platform to disability sport, as it would soon be rewarded. Disbelievers should watch the critically acclaimed film *Murderball*, which is about paraplegic full-contact rugby. It is not for the faint-hearted, though that is because of the ferocity of the contact, not the individual stories of the participants.

Although this column has made the following point before, it is worth repeating: our support for and our attitude to the Paralympics in 2012 will go a long way to measuring our humanity and maturity, not just our financial support for disabled athletes.

59

Sir Alex Ferguson must not be allowed to squirm out of touchline ban

October 2009

At last people are finally recognising the diversionary tactics of Britain's foremost football manager. Perhaps it is only because Sir Alex Ferguson's criticism of referee André Marriner, after Manchester United's loss to Liverpool last Sunday, comes so soon after his rant at Alan Wiley, but it is no less welcome for that. With Riley it was an allegation that he was physically not fit enough to referee at the top level and now it is Marriner's caution of United's Vidić and refusal to dismiss Liverpool's Jamie Carragher – none of which to a neutral observer have much weight.

The problem now rests with the Football Association, which will be acutely aware that a further charge for the latest comments will allow Ferguson to repeat his allegation that there is some form of witch-hunt against him; the answer to which is that if he didn't comment, there would be no quarry.

Ferguson's guilty plea should not have been leaked before his hearing, but this confuses matters and we are in danger of mistaking his plea for contrition and an admission of wrongdoing. However, unless he has gone beyond his public apology, he has not withdrawn the charge and admitted he was wrong. Also, by maintaining that he was raising a serious issue, so serious that it has not been raised by any of his Premier League counterparts, he is seeking to spin his words into a favourable context.

Let us revisit the facts; his original comments had no caveat that he was highlighting an issue by reference to Wiley; the comments were solely about Wiley. They were made publicly in an inappropriate forum and seemingly without research.

Wiley's fitness test results proved that the allegation was groundless, unless Ferguson was thereby alleging that all Premier League referees were unfit because the standards were generally too low.

An unqualified apology is what is needed, and, given that the allegation was wrong, Ferguson should not be allowed to introduce his spun version as mitigation. He did not raise a general point, and although this is unproven, the more credible explanation is simply that he was making another diversionary comment to stop his players being lambasted in the press.

Ferguson's advisers believe a touchline ban can be avoided by explaining his comments and relying on the fact that no manager has had a touchline ban for post-match comments. However, Ferguson has not apologised properly, has not withdrawn his wrongful allegation and is still spinning. These facts would allow the FA, if it has the desire and the bottle, to distinguish this case and therefore allow it to go beyond previous punishments.

Or is it going to be bamboozled by lawyers and lose sight of the facts? It is important that it does not, because that would also create a precedent.

60

Sporting stars brave public scorn to tackle depression

November 2009

'Stress? Don't make me laugh. Try being on £200 a week – that's stress.' You must have heard these or similar sentiments when a high-profile sporting figure is reported to be suffering from depression.

The BBC television programme *Inside Sport* made a valuable contribution to this subject. That it only scratched the topic's surface was inevitable, given its complexity, and while there was too little exploration of specifically what the sufferers faced and how the problem was treated, the fact that the programme got so many well-known athletes to discuss this most personal of issues was significant.

The contributors' tales will have drawn a mixed reaction from viewers, ranging from empathy to cynical dismissal and all degrees between, but one thing should have been common ground: the subject is too little understood and raised too infrequently.

Our attitude to depression has matured only to the extent that any reasonable person would admit that it can be an illness; beyond that, there is a wealth of anecdotes posing as evidence that shape perception, and which have led to unhelpfully vernacular judgements and utterings about the illness. Like many simple truths they are simplistic.

Above all, many criticisms have at their foundation an assertion, implicit or otherwise, that a sportsman's depression either is not real or is unjustifiable. What have they got to be depressed about? Can there be a prouder moment than pulling on your country's jersey? Being paid for doing something you love and acquiring fame to boot? The sufferers are ungrateful and weak-willed.

The 'man-on-£200-per-week' argument is flawed for the following reason. Suppose that in his town everyone earns £200 per week; our man is thus an average earner and can buy no more or less than his neighbour. On income alone he has no reason to feel any more stress or dissatisfaction over his lot than his neighbour.

The same is true of the man living in the next town, where everyone earns £20,000 per week. Only once each knows of the other's circumstances does income become an issue, and as such it cannot of itself be causative of any dissatisfaction.

Moreover, the man on £200 per week, who it is asserted lives the sort of life where he might be entitled to get depressed, is suddenly on the other end of the equation when you find a man earning £150 per week.

The truth is that income and status have only a partial bearing on the matter, and they are neither an inevitable precursor of, nor protection against, the illness.

'They just don't live in the real world' is another line often trotted out. Well, your real world is where you are, unless you are omnipresent. It depends on what you do in your real world and what you have to deal with as a result. The sportsman's world of glitterati, high earnings and fame is, to him, mundane, as are its pressures and stresses. That the majority of people do not inhabit it does not make it less real and the fact that there are circumstances involving equal or greater stress is irrelevant; Ronnie O'Sullivan and Neil Lennon cannot simultaneously be sportsmen and work on the bins.

To succeed at the highest sporting level an athlete must have willpower, discipline and self-reliance. If so, why do they suffer and why can they not use these qualities to sort out their problems?

John Kirwan, the most impressive sporting contributor to the programme, was right to point out that these qualities are used to achieve sporting ends and so are familiar to the athlete. They may be useful in combating stress and depression, but not until the person knows what he is suffering from and is taught how to treat it.

Many contributors pointed out that, unlike a broken leg, depression is not a visible illness and this is complicated by the fact that its symptoms vary widely, but they are no less real if they are mild or acute.

Frank Bruno was ill before he was sectioned, but it was not until that happened that the *Sun* newspaper was inclined to treat the subject seriously, and it is the same with a lot of people. Odd behaviour is laughed at or seen as eccentricity, until the sufferer does something dramatic and all too often harmful.

This glib approach to mental health adds to the stigma and fear of seeking help before the condition is advanced. It is obvious to anyone with a modicum of insight into the subject that Paul Gascoigne showed clear symptoms of obsessive-compulsive disorder throughout his schooldays. In his environment – the macho Geordie world of shipyards, football and Newky Brown – neither he nor his parents wanted him to be seen as doolally and his slide into illness is a Shakespearean tragedy.

Traditional British advice like 'pull yourself together' and 'keep a stiff upper lip' are about as useful as the on-field exhortation to 'sort it out'. Though nebulous and pointless, the instruction is still routinely issued by team-mates, even captains, and it never helps.

In the background to all this are the assumptions people, even seasoned commentators, make about the lot of the elite sportsman. Most do not see beyond the material riches, and even when they do they do not understand that with most positives comes a negative.

Playing in front of 80,000 people and being in the papers is thrilling, but brings with it a fear of failure and intrusion. Being unable to know what it is like, most assume it to be what they would like and so the problems continue.

More should have been heard from the impressive Dr Steve Peters. His simplified explanations of unusual stress in sport, and his obvious sympathy and yet practical approach to resolving associated problems, showed why he was a crucial part of British cycling's success at the Olympics in Beijing.

We need more Steve Peterses, more brave athletes, more discussion and less cynicism. It should not be thus, but if well-known figures can be used to alter our attitude to mental illness then thousands of 'ordinary' people who suffer similarly might find the courage to ask for help.

61

England players need to be removed from the FA Cup if winning the World Cup is what we want

November 2009

If the England football team reverse forty-four years of World Cup failure, as we all hope they do, it will be in spite of their fans and their governing bodies. When you compare the preparation of the football team for the World Cup 2010 against those of nearly every other sport, save cricket, you can see how badly they are hampered by various interested parties, none of whom is prepared to give much for the greater good.

The ideal preparation for a tournament like the World Cup is planned at least two, if not four years out, but if that is not possible, the final year is even more crucial in terms of delivering athletes at the peak of their performance cycle and as well prepared as possible to give them the best chance of success.

The World Cup starts on 11 June, with, in the month before, the final Premier League games, the FA Cup final and the Champions League final as late as 22 May. The relative strength of English club teams means it is perfectly possible for their international players to be involved in three successive dogfights.

Pre-tournament camp, rumoured to be in Austria, could have some players turning up with three weeks' rest and others two days after playing possibly the most important game of their careers to date.

Although club managers will try to give these players rest when they can, it is not satisfactory that the country's campaign relies on managers, who themselves will be under great pressure to play their best players.

As there is a 50 per cent chance of playing at altitude in the last-sixteen games and quarter-finals, Fabio Capello's pre-tournament camp in Austria is crucial.

If a player has experience of feeling short of breath or the strange lethargy that can overcome you at altitude, he will know what it is and will not add panic to the stress already on his body. In addition, the ball flies further; short passes arrive sooner and are more diffi-cult to control. Goalkeepers especially face a hard time because whipped-in crosses will be like tracer bullets on the high veld.

In contrast, the German team will have had a three-week break at Christmas and with a smaller league and only one cup com-petition will play far fewer games. In fitness terms this almost guarantees that they will be in better physical shape than their English counterparts.

Supposing at least one English club makes the Champions League final in Madrid, there will be twenty days before the World Cup kick-off.

The multiple media commitments of the England team – reporting to camp for pre-tournament fitness tests, medicals and administrative matters, kitting out and the like, travel and decamp-ing in Pezula Resort Hotel and Spa between Cape Town and Port Elizabeth – incredible as this sounds, will take the best part of four days without a ball being kicked in anger.

This gives only two weeks' concentrated time in camp before the off, three if they are drawn in groups F or G.

Saturday's friendly against Brazil in Qatar is dictated solely by the company to which the Brazilian FA has sold its commercial rights and the fact that England's players are shifted on to another flight to play in stifling heat amply demonstrates that commercial imperatives come before athletic ones.

Few fans would accept a truncated Premier League season, though they will shout loudly for Ingerland for the duration of the World Cup. As such, the FA could have dictated that England players or Premier League clubs should not take part in this year's FA Cup. This would have guaranteed another two weeks' rest and preparation time for England's World Cup players.

Given the shortfall in revenue likely because of this step, the Premier League could have been asked to make it up as the *quid pro quo* for their competition not being affected. That way the sacrifice would have been spread.

We are quick to claim we are patriotic; we chant it loudly and kiss the badge. When it comes to the sacrifice necessary for ensuring the best possible chance of success for our national team, the often ignored part of the definition of patriotism, putting your country's interests before your own, we will not do this – not patriotic at all.

Football's false indignation

Only a few weeks ago, sportswriters with a football background condemned rugby as a sink of depravity. It is true that the totally unacceptable was discovered, but let us consider rugby's response. The player involved – four-month ban; the coach – three-year ban; and an inquiry going back fifteen years to try to find similar nefariousness.

Cheating as per David Ngog's unsubtle dive has raised a fresh bout of breast-beating in football circles, but nothing will change. The solution is simple – retrospective citing and video evidence – but it won't be introduced. Therefore, if football has not the bottle to take the necessary steps, it should stop whingeing because this false indignation is becoming tedious.

62

Sport is better off without BBC's celebrity spin for its review of the year

December 2009

BBC's *Sports Personality of the Year* is unique as a two-hour multi-platform, multi-format live broadcast; something unequalled by any of its competitors, terrestrial or satellite. It is the one time in the year when the arts mafia, full of those who got picked last during games at school, are compelled to put the genre at the centre of its output.

Sport, with its unique place in British social history, and where class, race and background do not matter, has to fight for precious mainstream time. Why is there no dedicated sports channel? The success of Radio 5 Live provides ample evidence that it is both needed and justified. Sport could be on either BBC3 or BBC4, replacing programmes hardly anybody watches.

Though outstanding, not least in its ability to assemble so much talent, the show also has maddening flaws which were also apparent in the preview programme broadcast on Wednesday night, with its misguided attempts to 'broaden' its focus, and to appeal to the chronically indolent who watch reality TV.

Why add a bunch of soap stars and comics to the distinguished athletes who argued for each nominee? Of what aid in making your choice were comments such as 'People should vote for Jenson Button because he absolutely deserves it,' or 'I don't know whether to shake his hand or to kiss him'. For Ryan Giggs we had,

'He doesn't go to work; he goes to genius-world' – stunningly inapposite and banal.

These omnipresent polluters of every other TV genre are not needed because sport has more genuine drama, real news and real personalities, year after year. This idiotic obsession with celebrity lessened the preview with every word spoken by the non-sporting advocates.

Why should non-sports people not have their say? They do, when they vote, but when you want advice about building a house you ask an architect not an actor from *Rising Damp*. No doubt a gimmick will be introduced on the night to provide light relief for viewers from the MTV generation who are unable to concentrate on a single topic for more than a couple of minutes.

As for impossibly subjective decision, the name of the award itself makes things worse. Given the BBC's willingness to drop iconic sports themes and treasured brands, such as *Grandstand*, its reluctance to drop the word personality is ludicrous. The incluctable jibes about whether the winner actually possesses one are singularly unhelpful because that is expressly not one of the judgement criteria.

Early indications are that Button is favourite to lift the big prize but, even though his World Championship win was fantastic, the knowledge that he contributes about 20 per cent (as assessed by David Coulthard) to any race win must mean, in purely sporting terms, that he has achieved less than other nominees.

David Haye's case has been artificially boosted by hype that purposely suggests his world title win was a miracle because of his size difference with Nikolai Valuev. In reality he is champion at the lowest ebb of heavyweight boxing in history; not his fault, but it should be taken into account.

Any athlete from a team sport has an inherent difficulty in winning the award. How do you dissociate his contributions from those of his team-mates to any particular achievement? Probably the best you can do is look for his to have been the seminal reason for the success, for him to have been the outstanding player within the team at the time.

Giggs has not been the top player in his team for the last few seasons, despite achieving over a substantial time and winning more Premier League titles than anyone else. This, and the fact that he has not performed regularly on the international stage, mean he should not win; furthermore, if the length of achievement is sufficient to win, then he is even more worthy if he sees out another season with Manchester United. What is really needed is a new category for those who, like Giggs, show sustained excellence without necessarily being the principal star of their side.

The claims of the track and field athletes are fairly equal, but Jessica Ennis's heptathlon gold medal at the World Championships in Berlin was won with fewer points than the record held by Denise Lewis; Phillips Idowu's gold in the triple jump is a British but not a world record.

Gymnast Beth Tweddle and diver Tom Daley are the best Britons in the history of their sports, and were it not for the minority status of their disciplines they would be nearer the top of the bookies' lists.

For me, the claims of Andy Murray are almost conclusive. He is the best ever Briton, a winner and at one point reached No. 2 in the world this year in a sport that is arguably now stronger than at any time, including two players, Roger Federer and Rafael Nadal, acknowledged as some of tennis's greatest.

The fact that the name atop of my list isn't in the top ten shows how subjective the whole thing is – Tony McCoy. With more than three thousand wins he has sustained his excellence, is the best in his sport this year, riding in a dangerous sport and not just on one thing. I don't particularly like horse racing, but I am happy to salute greatness.

Speaking ill of Daniel James

December 2009

The *Daily Mail* told on Wednesday of how Matt King overcame catastrophic rugby injuries to gain a first-class degree and a training place with a top London firm of lawyers. It also chose to juxtapose Matt's bravery with the story of Daniel James who, the newspaper stressed, suffered less severe injuries – and his decision to visit the Dignitas Clinic, where his suicide was assisted.

The moral judgement made not only in the way Andrew Levy's stories were set out on the page, but also by the headlines 'The boy who never gave up' as against 'The boy who didn't want to live', indicates a deplorable moral position over an issue of personal choice; one which is the business of nobody else.

I'll bet that Matt King passes no judgement on Daniel James; so what right has Levy to do this?

International Rugby Board ignoring evidence of a game in turmoil

December 2009

Background

In 2003, rugby union was increasingly popular. Yet, despite this, an IRB group called the Forward Thinking Group, in the nebulous belief that it had a duty to continually look at ways to improve the game, decided to embark on a full-scale review of rugby's laws, and proposed thirty-five experimental law variations. None of the Unions comprising the governing board of the IRB consulted their constituents about whether, what or how this should be done.

In 2006, a body called the Law Advisory Committee (LAC) was created to run the trials which took place over the next three years. The following statement accompanied the LAC's creation; even with three years to identify the same, the IRB could not specify any serious problem areas, nor name what laws were said to need improvement.

The IRB is conscious that any changes must take into account their successful application within the professional and recreational areas of the Game. The IRB has no desire whatsoever to change the traditional fabric of the Game that has made it such a popular international Game.

That said, most people associated with the Game, including spectators, would agree that the sport is in a very healthy state but that there are some fundamental problems creep-ing in. The Game is quicker, players are stronger and faster, contact is more aggressive and physical, and the advance-ment of skill levels is putting a strain on the Laws themselves in terms of the contest for possession. There is an underly-ing consensus that Rugby does need a thorough review in terms of the Laws of the Game.

The last sentence is particularly disingenuous: there was no such consensus at any time from inception to end. In fact, only the RFU consulted all levels within its own Union. A few Unions can-vassed limited comments and some not at all – hardly a consensus. What must also be kept firmly in mind is that any changes would apply to all levels of rugby, 95 per cent of which is not professional.

What followed was a lesson in how not to conduct such exper-iments. None of the experienced men responsible for all this has given a comprehensible explanation, particularly of why they failed to spot what to everyone else were glaring deficiencies and mistakes.

For no apparently urgent reason, rugby union was subject to an experiment, the like of which no other sport would attempt (for good reasons) and one which did positive harm; it set man against man and exposed the game to ridicule around the world.

In 2009, all but a handful of minor law changes were aborted. Nobody ever said sorry and nobody was sacked for what hap-pened.

Just five years ago there was nothing much wrong with rugby, but the latest International Rugby Board statistics point to a broken game with too much emphasis on kicking.

In 2004 the International Rugby Board reported that there were an average of 4.5 tries a game in the Six Nations Championship and 5.2 in the Tri-Nations. There were 4.6 and 6.0

penalty goals on average and the ball was in play 46 and 43 per cent of the time respectively. There were 291 passes per Six Nations game and 251 in the Tri-Nations, with 57 and 50 kicks.

There were no complaints, yet the IRB introduced thirty-five experimental law variations which it now says were only ever options, to be taken or left as wanted. Such 'blue-sky' thinking caused three years of argument and turmoil.

The 2009 autumn internationals were plagued by breakdown mayhem and aerial kick-tennis. Southern hemisphere fans say 'It's your own fault; you killed the ELVs.' Some blame lack of ambition, pointing to New Zealand's and Australia's final games as proof that the game works as it is.

They are wrong, of course. Poor play and the adopted ELV penalising the return of the ball into the twenty-two are contributors to the try drought. There is also a major problem at the breakdown. In combination these factors mean many teams, including the world and Tri-Nations champions South Africa, base their game on kicking.

This year's Six Nations/Tri-Nations statistics, which include the two teams held up as exemplars of ambition, show the problem is global: tries 3.7/3.0; penalty goals 4.9/7.7; ball in play 49 per cent/42 per cent; passes 273/222; kicks 65/60.

The 2009 IRB review states that in the first Lions Test South Africa made only forty-nine passes and their hooker passed as many times as the fly-half. They won the Tri-Nations by making fewest breakdowns, least passes and having most kicks. In one game their forty-three passes was the lowest by any team in either competition for seven years.

The IRB's only response has been to enshrine the controversial breakdown ruling as law, making it irreversible until after the 2011 World Cup. That is bad enough but what terrifies is that they intend to review the laws in 2011 with a Laws Consultation Group assessing global playing trends. As before, no specifics, just a wide spectrum to indulge fertile but misguided minds.

Sorry, the IRB have done something else – they agreed to waste money trialling Goalscan technology to see whether a kick at goal goes over. When has this been an issue? What most fans do not know is that behind this obstinacy is a desperate attempt to avoid further public derision.

Following a survey which highlighted the breakdown retention rate of 95 per cent in the 2007 World Cup final (over that tournament as a whole it was 92 per cent) one leading IRB official called the figures 'truly scary'. The IRB and ill-informed commentators said it would lead to the game being for only one shape and size of player.

They then, wrongly, assumed that the high retention rate meant there could not be proper competition for the ball at the breakdown and ruled in favour of the defender, thereby overlooking the crucial fact that quality and speed of ball is determined by what competition does take place, even when the defence does not make a turnover. A high retention rate is not a problem provided there is the possibility of turnovers. Rugby league outlaws competition for the ball in the tackle, unless one on one, balancing this by allowing a maximum six possessions before the ball is turned over to the opponents.

If the retention rate almost guaranteed the attacking side would score there would be no problem, but is does not. The reverse is true; the more phases a team have to win, the fewer the chances of scoring. Most tries occur after three or fewer breakdowns.

The IRB also ignored evidence showing that in the 1970s matches averaged around fifty breakdowns, attracting six or seven attackers and five or six defenders. Today's games have between 150 and 190 breakdowns, attracting 3.3 attackers and just 1.2 defenders. This is why there is no space.

All the above have made kicking the most effective tactical option. It is facile to say all you need is a fly-half to play flat; what if you do not have a Dan Carter or Matt Giteau? And why were they not successful in this year's Tri-Nations?

Rather than admit causing this mess, the IRB blames teams for lacking ambition.

Identifying your most effective way of playing and winning is normally praised. Why should a team refuse this option in favour of entertaining when they know their opponents are not similarly compelled?

The greatest problem is making more space and this means committing more players to the breakdown. Why refuse to look at how this was done in the 1970s? I'll tell you why – it would mean reintroducing rucking; the love that dare not speak its name.

The study of history is important to avoid repeating mistakes. The IRB should go back to school.

65

Tiger Woods bashing is based on old-fashioned jealousy

December 2009

Tiger Woods's family are the only victims of his recent scandals. He deserves the criticism befitting a married man with two young children who has allegedly had multiple affairs; as he is a high-profile figure this scrutiny is public.

He does not, however, deserve ignorant, self-righteous lecturing from all quarters. He is a role model; set himself up as a family man; Mr Goody Two-Shoes; advertises products, blah blah blah.

I don't recall the Woods family featuring in his endorsements, and whether those brands retain him is their business. I don't remember him ever saying that he was better than anyone else, apart from on the golf course, where he certainly is. As for the family man, I don't recall Tiger Woods posing with his family and asking anyone to trust him with high office. It is certainly true that many a journalist wrote of Woods that he had it all, was the embodiment of the American dream and mentioned that he was a family man.

Ah yes, they say, but he did nothing to disabuse us of this idyllic view. Well, what is he supposed to do when that is written – go into print and deny it? How would that go down and, given the millions of words written for profit off his back, how could it be achieved practically anyway?

That he is a role model may well be true but he is caught either way. What would be the reaction if he refused to be pictured with children or eschewed charity work involving youngsters? Who does he think he is? How effective would be any protestation that this was because at some time he might mess up and it would be held against him?

He is the world's top golfer – so what? Is a higher moral standard expected of the top physicist, archaeologist, Fleet Street editor? No: behind a lot of the bashings is good old-fashioned jealousy. It's just so unfair that one man can have all that talent and all that money; if I can't have it why should he?

His family problems do not interest me beyond noting that they must be agonising for the innocent members of his family; they are their problems and what kind of person delights in the downfall of others?

And then we get to the personal. He's boring, the clichéd comment from journalists who have never even met him. He plays in a boring manner.

Well, only to the stupid, who believe the ability to fire long iron shots to the heart of the green consistently is such. This description of his play is stupefying to anyone with even a smidgen of sporting knowledge.

66

Gay rugby players have nothing to fear from following Gareth Thomas's lead

December 2009

Private Eye might cover it thus: Shock Horror – Rugby Player says 'I'm not Gay'.

Arwel Davies-Jones, the fearsome, burly Pontypotty captain and prop, yesterday broke down in a press conference and admitted that he was not gay. Fighting back the tears, Davies-Jones said, 'It's been such a strain; when all the boys josh in the afternoons, discussing fashion and background colour schemes, I used to join in and pretend that I liked rearranging furniture. But deep down, in my soul, I longed to be at the bar, drinking four gallons of Shane's bitter, running round a bar stool and staggering into a wall while singing "Delilah".'

He went on: 'I didn't like going down Old Compton Street in Soho when we played our away games in London, but that was the done thing and although I get severe hay fever, I would make a point to be first on to Hampstead Heath for training runs before games.' Continuing to explain, he said, 'I knew I was living a lie and I hated it.'

After years of turmoil the fearless and proud Valleys boy appears to have reached a point of no return. 'In the end I just said "To hell with it" and I thought if they don't like the fact that I whistle at women from the cab of my 4 x 4 Hummer, while blasting out gangsta rap; if they don't accept that I like

Rocky movies and not *Priscilla Queen of the Desert* then so be it.'

Those witnessing this brave act of confession were quick to reassure Davies-Jones ('Welly' to his mates) that he would not be an object of derision in rugby because frankly nobody bothers about his sexuality.

And so it was when I was asked by various forms of media to comment on Gareth Thomas coming out as gay; I replied that I couldn't care less. Like referee Nigel Owens (no longer the only official gay in the village), Thomas will hopefully find out that the rest of rugby also says 'so what?'.

Sorry, there is one point that registers emotionally and that is sadness that Thomas appears to have been troubled for so long and I hope any other gay players do not similarly worry about coming out; we really don't care.

Some have made a big thing out of Thomas's revelations and as the first international rugby union player to come out this is of note, but, frankly, in today's world did anybody doubt there were and are gay rugby players? Hopefully we are approaching the point where this sort of story will not fill the columns and the people involved will only be classed as heroes or villains for things they do on the field; a civilised state of affairs where someone's sexuality cannot be exploited for good or ill.

67

Invictus's long walk to telling the truth about 1995 Rugby World Cup

January 2010

Invictus, a film starring Morgan Freeman and Matt Damon, is released in Britain on 5 February. It is the story of Nelson Mandela's early struggles to unite his country, seen through the prism of the Springbok team's preparation for, and eventual winning of, the World Cup in 1995.

One critic, David Ansen, has written that the story is 'one that would be hard to believe if it were fiction. The wonder of *Invictus* is that it actually went down this way.' It is still too early to assess the true significance of that triumph and the part rugby played in the unification of post-apartheid South Africa but nobody should doubt that its influence was real.

Due to the relative stability of South Africa today, recollections often fail to record that at the time this success was far from certain. I toured South Africa in 1994 and played in the World Cup a year later and took the time to speak about the political situation with a variety of people of all races and political hues. The consensus was that they had reached the point where initial euphoria at rule by the black majority had been replaced with a realisation of how difficult would be the task of satisfying their expectations. The phrase 'knife edge' was used more than once.

As with most films based on actual events, this will manipulate a number of things to ensure what its makers consider a coherent narrative. For example, the publicity blurb inaccurately portrays the Springboks as also-rans before the tournament and ignores the reality that they were one of a number of teams entering the competition with the advantage of training and playing on a semi-professional basis.

Not having seen the film, it will be interesting to see if it mentions a number of the controversial incidents that have now been largely forgotten: the indirect claims by New Zealand that their players were poisoned and their sleep was deliberately interrupted before the final as well as the speech of Louis Luyt, the then president of South African rugby, which was so disgustingly triumphalist it embarrassed the Springboks, who apologised to the other teams.

One fact I hope is not distorted is the way in which the Springboks, captained by François Pienaar, only gradually won the backing of the black population; it was not there in 1994 nor when the tournament started. It was a memorable experience to witness the growing tide of support and belief, both in the team and the notion that its success could unite previously murderous opponents.

Another critic, Vince Mancini, has written, 'Bottom line, in a movie like this, where we know essentially how the plot's going to play out just from watching the trailer, the key is charisma, and none of the rugby players have it.'

He may be correct about charisma, but only in so far as it relates to the genre of film. Character is the key in both sport and politics, as both Nick Faldo and Margaret Thatcher amply demonstrated. Mandela has both qualities and Pienaar has the latter in abundance.

It is commonly assumed that sport's true greats must be interesting, articulate and so on; people are quick to denigrate sporting achievements by highlighting personal defects. That Pienaar might not be in your top ten dinner party guests is supremely irrelevant when you consider his seminal role in this tale. It is frequently forgotten that courage was displayed by white, as well as black, South Africans in overcoming the prejudice within a game traditionally synonymous with white minority government.

In sport there is more than enough true drama for any film; the problem is that few directors ever capture the spirit of events that are intrinsically immediate. Further, it is usually not the players who are lacking, it is the actors. It is not enough to mimic just the demeanour. Hardly any actors make plausible sportsmen because they can rarely emulate the essential part of a sportsman's character that is shown in a pass, a stroke or a punch. Daniel Day-Lewis came close in *The Boxer*, as did Robert De Niro in *Raging Bull*. Richard Harris didn't pull it off in *This Sporting Life* and Sylvester Stallone was a mile away in all the *Rocky* films.

If *Invictus* can convey anything approaching the taut and vaguely menacing atmosphere before and during that World Cup, it will have done well. Freeman may get close to a plausible impression of Mandela, but Damon has the harder task in trying to play Pienaar.

However, at least Damon's general intelligence and social awareness give him a chance: his acerbic criticism of Sarah Palin's recent candidacy for the American vice-presidency was not only succinct, it was more devastating than any made by a political critic. François would have approved.

68

Bill McLaren – quite simply a genius

January 2010

I am one of the privileged few to have both been commented on and commentated with the late, great Bill McLaren and in both respects it was a pleasure and an honour.

Listening as a boy to the rich brogue that accompanied every rugby international, it was beyond my dreams to think that one day it would be applied to me and when it happened I played and replayed Bill's first mention of my name in a Calcutta Cup game. Somehow my first cap felt all the more real for having that voice pronounce that it was so.

Few commentators have so thoroughly penetrated not just the coverage of their game but also, by their contributions, shaped the ethos and atmosphere within it. From the lowliest junior XV to the changing rooms of international teams there was not one that did not have someone at some time produce their mimicry of McLaren's comments.

The first time I worked with him I was even more nervous than usual. He was, after all, the stuff of legend. But it was more than that: I didn't want to let him down. Bill didn't give much in the way of advice but he would guide you through by the manner in which he brought in natural pauses where you could contribute.

And – very important when there is a match commentator and co-commentator – he never strayed from his job of description and trespassed on your area of explanation or comment. He was kind enough to say that he thought my first attempt had been 'handsome', leaving the memorable parting shot that 'you didn't repeat anything I said and nor what the viewers could see for themselves'.

Among the many comments following Bill's passing have been recommendations that would-be commentators should study tapes of his performances, the idea being that they could learn all they needed to know by doing just that. I disagree. Aspiring broadcasters should only do this if they keep a few important points firmly in mind.

The most seductive aspect of the way Bill worked was that it appeared effortless. A proportion of it was, because he was blessed with natural talent, but what went unseen was the enormous amount of preparation required to augment this, to the point where it seemed anyone could do it.

His tremendously inventive way of describing all aspects of rugby might tempt beginners to try to follow suit. This would never work because Bill's descriptions were entirely spur-of-the-moment, each one a nugget. Without this innate ability to create the legendary, any follower would be bound to fail.

Where his technical excellence was apparent – and this should be an aspiration of all who work in that role – was his mastery at instantly identifying players. In a fast-moving game where there are often tangled limbs and many bodies this is not easy but I doubt Bill made more than a handful of mistakes in this regard in his whole career.

His warm, positive style of commentary would not have fitted much longer with the younger public's desire for harder scrutiny of performances from highly paid professionals. Now probably only Peter Alliss still carries a sport in this way. Bill said as much at the last game I did with him, another Calcutta Cup at Murrayfield, and I think he was happier not to be involved in the new style of analysis and comment.

Among all the many memories I have of him one thought stays with me: Bill absolutely loved rugby and rugby absolutely loved him. He will be missed and he is an impossible act to follow. How many men leave that sort of mark on the world?

69

FIFA's Thierry Henry handball verdict shows wilful disregard for its own core values

January 2010

By failing to punish Thierry Henry for his World Cup handball against the Republic of Ireland, FIFA has undermined its own mission statement.

The FIFA official mission statement is full of grandiose claims. One says: 'Integrity. We believe that, just as the game itself, FIFA must be a model of fair play, tolerance, sportsmanship and transparency.' It is signed by Joseph S. Blatter, FIFA's president.

On 2 December, the FIFA executive committee asked the disciplinary committee to analyse the handling offence committed by Thierry Henry during the France v. Republic of Ireland match on 18 November, and to consider the possible disciplinary consequences.

Following its meeting on 18 January, FIFA said that its disciplinary committee had reached the conclusion that there was no legal foundation for the committee to consider the case because handling the ball cannot be regarded as a serious infringement as stipulated in article 77a) of the FIFA disciplinary code. There is no other legal text that would allow the committee to impose sanctions for any incidents missed by match officials.

Can anyone square this wilful inaction with the core value claimed in FIFA's mission statement? Can anyone, other than

Blatter, seriously argue that the Henry incident, which cannot be divorced from its context, was not serious and that it clearly runs counter to FIFA's alleged model of fair play? The only people capable of rationalising the irrational are the cowards who sit at football's top table. For them, black can be white, or indeed any colour they choose, because the rest of the footballing world has no say.

FIFA is as opaque and unaccountable as the European Commission and shares the same disregard for democracy and application of its own rules. Jerome Champagne, FIFA's director of international relations and a potential force for good, has been sacked.

So, when the World Cup 2010 kicks off in South Africa – amid the unavoidable self-congratulation and trite parroting of the phrase 'the beautiful game' – we should remind ourselves that the men on screen are the same craven bunch who cannot bring themselves to stand for what is right when it all becomes too inconvenient.

70

FIA's staggering incompetence makes it a laughing stock

January 2010

Even for a sport that seems unable to conduct itself in anything approaching a normal fashion, one in which threat and counter-threat, conspiracy and litigation are routine, the latest staggering event takes some beating.

A French court has overturned the lifetime and five-year bans on Flavio Briatore and Pat Symonds, respectively, which were handed out by the Fédération Internationale de l'Automobile (FIA), Formula One's ruling body. In so doing, the court appears to have uncovered the inconvenient facts that not only did the FIA not apply proper procedure, it also did not have the jurisdiction to give the bans in the first place because neither Briatore nor Symonds was a FIA licence holder and therefore subject to FIA rules.

The charges followed an internal investigation by Renault which suggested that Briatore, their former team principal, Nelson Piquet Jnr, their former driver, and Symonds, their former executive director of engineering, conspired for Piquet to crash out of the Singapore Grand Prix deliberately to enhance the race prospects of Renault's lead driver, Fernando Alonso.

When the allegations surfaced from Piquet Jnr, Briatore denied any knowledge of the instruction and threatened legal action against Piquet and his father, the former world champion. Briatore and Symonds also chose not to contest charges brought by the FIA and both resigned from Renault five days before the World Motor Sport Council sat in judgement on 21 September – a strange way of asserting your innocence.

The differential sentences handed down took into account Symonds's acceptance that he took part in the conspiracy and the fact that he told the WMSC that it was to his 'eternal regret and shame' that he participated in the conspiracy.

Briatore, despite the evidence against him, then claimed that former FIA president Max Mosley was 'blinded by an excessive desire for personal revenge' in pursuing the case and further asserted that Mosley 'assumed the roles of complainant, investigator, prosecutor and judge', claiming the case against him was a breach of the 'most basic rules of procedure and the rights to a fair trial'.

Briatore has now said, 'The decision handed down restores to me the dignity and freedom that certain people had arbitrarily attempted to deprive me of.' He added that it was too early for him to talk about returning to F1. 'Let me take a little time to enjoy this moment of happiness after this difficult period,' he said.

We therefore have a situation whereby one man who admitted his guilt remains undisciplined and another who, at best, still has not refuted the evidence against him, is now taking the high moral ground because of the complete incompetence of a ruling body. That the FIA was incompetent was not in dispute before this ludicrous affair. That it did not ensure all people involved in its sport were bound by its rules and was not even able to apply those rules properly now exposes it as a complete joke, probably the worst governing body in sport.

To the extent that Mosley was responsible for this, he deserves to go down as one of the worst administrators of all time. Faced with the most serious charges ever brought, in possession of an admission from Symonds and apparently overwhelming evidence, they still cocked it up. Do you laugh or cry?

Mind you, when people are involved with anomalous views like those of Bernie Ecclestone, F1's commercial rights holder, perhaps we should not be surprised. Four days after the FIA verdict, having sat on the sanctioning body, he advised Briatore to appeal against his own decision, saying, 'It was quite harsh on Flavio. I don't think it was necessary but I was on the commission so I'm as guilty as anybody [of passing the sentence].'

After the court verdict Ecclestone said of Briatore, 'I don't know if he wants to come back and, if he did, how he would. The biggest problem . . . is if you are arrested for murder, you go to court but you are still branded a murderer, even if you get off.' Ecclestone continued, 'If I was president of the FIA, I'd call Flavio and say, "Let's have a chat. Maybe we were a little bit over the top and sorry that you have had to take the attitude you have taken, and let's try and repair things."'

But Ecclestone also said, 'It's not over by a long way. Just because a bloody judge has said what he's said doesn't make any difference . . . The court said it was wrong, so the FIA can start all over again . . . and it will go on and on.' Er, no Bernie, the court did not say that Briatore had not done the things alleged, it said he wasn't bound by the rules. Briatore never went to court in the proper sense and no judicial body has got him off the substantive charges.

Moreover, there is no room for this over-the-top nonsense. If Briatore did what he was accused of, the FIA's sentence was not excessive, though it still should have been reached and applied properly. If not, it should not have gone ahead with the prosecution in the first place.

For what reason are the participants in F1 happy to accept this sort of intolerable nonsense? Surely it is time for a wholesale revision of the FIA and its procedures, and to say to Bernie, 'Thanks

for all you have done, but it's time to go for a long lie in the sun.'
That or send for the men in white coats.

Alternatively, let us have the teams themselves running the
sport and an end to the personal fiefdoms of those whose time has
come and gone. This is not just for the sake of F1, it is for the
good of sport as a whole.

English clubs jumped into bed with big business years ago – don't cry foul now

January 2010

Football clubs are torn between two worlds: that of corporate greed and also being a community and cultural asset.

There are thousands of petitions lodged electronically on www.number10.gov.uk; some are serious, others silly and many impossibly ambitious. Andrew Henderson's petition is unusual in that it concurrently manages to be all three of these when it states: 'We, the undersigned, petition the Prime Minister to believe the Government should urgently take action on behalf of all football supporters to prevent Manchester United Football Club (and other English football clubs) being destroyed by corporate greed.'

Debt in business is a serious issue, though when the topic was raised in a relatively mild fashion by Lord Triesman, of the Football Association, a few months ago it brought howls of indignation from the Premier League executives and stupid was one of the more polite epithets hurled the way of the noble lord.

The problem is that while it is correct that many businesses do trade with debts, football does not know where to position itself *vis-à-vis* the corporate world. Depending on who you speak to, you will get a variety of views, but what they essentially come down to: it is a business, or it is a business but it is also cultural and clubs are community and national assets.

As a result the application of proper business structures and adoption of accepted practices is ignored when convenient. The income/wages ratio is only one instance of football departing from sound principles; to this you could add many more.

Any businessman will tell you that when a disproportionately large part of your income comes from one source it is unwise to assume and spend on the basis that this is guaranteed, yet virtually no club's business plan operates with a contingency reserve of each year's revenue.

Similarly, forecasts reliant on highly subjective assumptions like winning or qualifying for certain tournaments would not be accepted in normal businesses without there also being an alternative strategy worked out as well.

At the same time football is quite capable of using the phrase 'well, football is a business these days and in business you have to make hard choices' when unpopular measures such as varying kick-off times and fixtures or hugely expensive merchandising cause complaint.

Football is more than just business but it entered into that arena of its own volition and accepts the benefits; it cannot then protest when it is afflicted by the difficulties that doing business also brings.

When Manchester United went public in 1991, the club entered the big world of business and with a valuation of just £47 million. It was very small beer indeed; this isn't even in the upper echelons of the Alternative Investment Market, the London Stock Exchange's international market for smaller companies. Those involved understood – or should have – the ramifications of this decision for the club as a business and a sporting entity. Football, with its myriad businessmen running all ninety-two league clubs, should have been likewise informed.

In turnover terms United is still not a medium Footsie 100 company and is dangerously leveraged. The club's demise would be mourned, but the consequences would be nowhere near as serious as those caused by the disasters at Marconi or Equitable

Life. In the case of the latter, people lost their jobs, savings and pensions and did so in far greater numbers.

We must also presume that what is being requested is that United's status is maintained, not just their survival; which is akin to the attitude of those Lloyd's names assuming their privileged existence was in some way a right, when their investments suddenly didn't produce the annual fat cheque.

Were intervention to take place by way of financial support there would undoubtedly be an outcry from the majority of tax-payers who have no interest in the game, national though it may be. There would also be calls for aid to be withheld unless football clubs also accepted that they had to fall into line with everyone else and eschew practices which would be laughable in any other business sector.

Hardly any revenue is used for development of capital, and the equivalent of research and development through academies is not a priority. Why should anyone support a business model that is geared principally to enriching, beyond the dreams of avarice, only a few employees, while leaving it chronically underfunded in other areas and without commensurate shareholder reward?

Among the supporting paragraphs to the petition is a demand for help to prevent so-called investors bleeding clubs dry. Asset-stripping and hostile takeovers are common business practices. They have been the basis of many a fortune and are often rewarded in the Honours Lists. When you have taken the corporate shilling what right do you have to protection from these? Moreover, you could justifiably allege that it is the players' rapacious demands for a disproportionate percentage of a club's income that are equally bleeding the club dry.

Football's travails are not the business of Government and what are the petitioners proposing: a change in corporate law that applies to their interests alone? If they want to petition, the better target would be the Premier League because revised rules about fitness of owners and the type of finance they wish to introduce could be introduced without trying to make impossible changes to the law, with all the time and expense involved over what is essentially a private issue.

If financial Armageddon does occur, football will survive, albeit in a different guise. In doing so it might rid itself of many of the excesses it indulges and it could be argued that it might rediscover some of the values that have been lost in the race for cash.

Maybe this is the time for the game to take a look at what it has become and where it is going and, though it goes against the grain, to admit that on this point Messrs Blatter and Platini are right: clubs do need to balance the books and not live above their means.

72

Superbowl – it really is the greatest show on earth

January 2010

On Sunday Superbowl XLIII, the planet's most watched domestic sport final, will have few followers in Britain, but they will be fanatics.

My passion for American Football began in 1982 and remains undimmed.

For many it is stop-start; too complicated, or, at three hours, too long. Yet no more so than cricket, which lasts anything from three hours to five days. American Football requires study: the more you understand, the more you enjoy.

There is no better-run, more professional game on earth, and this applies to the governing body, the National Football League and its teams, coaches, players and referees.

Attention to detail sets this game apart. The NFL indisputably runs the game, but consults the teams who, thereafter, get in line or are swiftly compelled to do so. It is unafraid of technology, and its officials, thus aided, rarely make mistakes. This ensures games are not won arbitrarily. On-field discipline is maintained by personal foul penalties, and repetition sees an offender out of the game; no argument.

Its broadcasting is of the highest order, with John Madden possibly the best commentator in any sport.

Facilities at every stadium are matched in the UK only by

Wembley and the Millennium Stadium. Fans sit unsegregated, drinking and eating, served by an army of enthusiastic concessionary staff capable of dealing with more than one person every five minutes.

Often decried as a softer version of rugby, because of its protective padding, critics fail to appreciate the sheer size of the men who play and the ferocity with which they assail each other. The average offensive guard weighs 323 pounds – 23 stone – and can run 100 yards in just over 12 seconds. An average quarterback is 6 foot 3 inches, weighs 16 stone and can throw the ball 70 metres.

The wide receivers, who catch passes, are outstanding athletes. To give some rough comparison, the NFL draft has a series of tests: 40-yard dash, bench press x 100 kg, vertical jump and broad jump. Justin Gatlin, the USA Olympic sprinter, dashed in 4.42 seconds, pushed 12 reps and had 40½-inch vertical and 11-foot long jumps. Eddie Royal from Virginia Tech, a college player just hoping to get picked by an NFL team out of many others, scored: 4.39; 24 reps; 36-inch vertical and 10.04 long jumps.

The main season is sixteen games, but the game's appalling attrition rate is demonstrated by the fact that the average NFL career is about three and a half seasons.

Rewards for top players are good by normal standards: the highest paid players in the league can make $7–8 million (£10 million) per year – similar to Premiership players. However, the average salary last year was $1.1 million (£16,000 per week), considerably less than the said footballers.

When you try to record your memories of twenty-five years of a sport, it is strange what jumps out at you. William Perry, 'The Fridge'; the courage of John Elway, the Denver Broncos quarterback, hurling himself through defensive players to gain a crucial 'first and goal' which eventually led to him lifting the Superbowl; the astonishing running of Barry Sanders in an otherwise average Detroit Lions team.

Possibly because it was so dramatically captured on film, my most vivid memory is of the horrific leg injury suffered by Washington Redskins' quarterback Joe Theisman, when sacked by New York Giants' linebacker Lawrence Taylor. Anybody recalling Danny Cipriani's injury will shudder when I say that Theisman's injury, replayed repeatedly, was far more graphic and gruesome.

This weekend's game in Tampa is between outsiders, the Arizona Cardinals, and favourites, the Pittsburgh Steelers. Wimbledon v. Liverpool might be an FA Cup final equivalent. The Steelers have the best defence in the NFL, and the cliché is that defence win games, especially against a run-based offence. However, the Cardinals have the second best passing game and, with three receivers in form, can bypass the trench warfare. They also have a former Superbowl MVP, Kurt Warner, to orchestrate their air attack – if they can stop Pittsburgh savaging him.

This one may go to the wire. I can't wait.

73

It is only right that John Terry
loses the England captaincy

February 2010

'Liquidator', by Harry J Allstars, is the track habitually played at Stamford Bridge just before the teams run out. When Manchester City are the visitors in three weeks' time, they might consider a blast of the Offspring song 'Come Out and Play (Keep 'Em Separated)'. On second thoughts, as the latter contains the lyrics 'Hey man, you disrespecting me, take him out', it is probably better to stick to the traditional tune; there will be no need to stoke the atmosphere when John Terry and Wayne Bridge face each other.

Disrespect is a relatively recently popularised phrase and is now used by people to cover such a wide variety of behaviour that it has wrongly become universal vernacular for anything that offends the accuser, but its more restricted meaning is one which is central to the debate taking place on Terry's captaincy of England and Chelsea.

The recent High Court ruling which overturned Terry's injunction allowed the publication of the details of Terry's affair with Bridge's former girlfriend, Vanessa Perroncel, and as a result the media are having a field day.

I do not subscribe to the claim that sportsmen, even those made captain of their country, forego the right to a certain amount of privacy. The sanctimonious cant about Tiger Woods was nothing more than weak justification for trying to hunt down any piece of titillating detail of his extramarital activities. However, in the case of Terry there are differences which mean we are right in discussing the effects, but not the minutiae, of his affair with Perroncel.

At the Bridge there is a sense of vicarious victimisation for Terry. Some of this is the short-sightedness displayed by many fans when it is one of their own caught behaving in a way that they would condemn if it was a player from a rival club; some of it comes from good old-fashioned class politics. Among the popular claims are that if Terry was not a lad from Dagenham the injunction would not have been lifted; that it does not matter what he does as long it doesn't affect the team; or, in some cases, that he is such a legend it doesn't matter what he does as long as he doesn't leave.

To those who say it does not matter, do you honestly think that? Do you set no boundaries? And as an aside, Terry is not a downtrodden worker, he is a fabulously wealthy and influential man sufficiently financed and advised so as to obtain the injunction in the first place.

Some support from ex-professionals has also been forthcoming, with one radio pundit erroneously claiming that, save for illegal behaviour, anything Terry did in his private life was irrelevant to his positions with club and country. He went further in claiming, again wrongly, that save for a bit of banter, the lads in the changing room would think nothing of it and that should Bridge find himself in the same England changing room as Terry he would be sufficiently professional not to cause trouble. When challenged on these claims he resorted to asking 'How many professional football club changing rooms have you been in?'

All of which neatly demonstrates the fact that so unremarkable has become aberrant behaviour in and out of the game that, for some, only criminality is deemed beyond the pale.

One of the primary considerations is that this latest escapade is merely the latest of a number in which Terry appears to show either that he has no idea of the concept of respect, or does, but doesn't care. At the root of his fine for drunken abuse and taunting of American tourists in the wake of the 9/11 outrage; getting kicked out of a nightclub for urinating in a beer glass and dropping the contents on the floor; parking his Bentley in a disabled bay; assisting a ticket tout to conduct a £10,000 tour of Chelsea's private training complex, and sleeping with a friend's ex-partner, is the attitude that because of who he is he can do what he wants. A facet of the 'don't you know who I am' culture.

Everybody makes mistakes and does things they regret, but the number and pattern of Terry's errors cannot be excused by using the human frailty defence. Furthermore, it is not being suggested that he is deprived of his place in any team, rather that the role of captain is not fitted by a person who continually fails to have respect for others.

Leaving aside the relationship with the wider public, it is facile to state that his most recent misdemeanours will not affect the dressing room. While players do try to be professional, being human they also have opinions and some have principles. Believe it or not, some will not find it acceptable that Terry has been unfaithful, but will not condemn him because it is outside the dressing room. They will take a different view of adultery with a team-mate's ex-partner: there are some things you just don't do.

Where is the respect shown by Terry to them when he allows voyeurs to secretly watch them as they relax unguarded; in having sex with a team-mate's ex-partner and one publicly claimed to be a good friend? Would you, could you, blithely overlook this?

Captaincy is an honour, as Terry himself stated on his elevation to both roles, but with that comes responsibility, not just opportunity, and often captaining a side means forgoing rather than indulging. Many famous captains speak of the need to lead by example, but they do not limit this to their behaviour on the field.

This is not a judgement regarding Terry's private sex life, but it is and should be a moral finding about what are our standards for captaincy.

Finally, it is right that the club have given Terry leave to try to rescue his marriage, but when he isn't even available as a consequence of his acts, how is it possible to say they do not affect the team?

My flawless debut as a referee

February 2010

You don't expect to be nervous when you're not playing; after all, you don't have fourteen team-mates you can disappoint. So why were the butterflies flitting about before a game between Rosslyn Park Nomads and a London Scottish XV? Maybe because as a referee I realised I could disappoint all thirty players, any spectators and then there was the little matter of the TV crew and several snappers. OK, the media presence is not something that afflicts the average referee, but the responsibility for the game as an event is something that is in his hands and is a significant difference from partaking in as a player.

Take, for just one example, the pre-match period. As a player all you have to concentrate on is putting on your kit and thinking about what you need to do while warming up. As a referee you have to manage that period by liaising with teams, the medical staff, your assisting officials, and the groundsman, ensuring each person is aware of what they need to do in this period and during and after the game.

I don't imagine many spectators or players ever question whether the ball is the regulation size and weight, the pitch is correctly marked or that there are the correct number of players on the field at kick-off – I certainly didn't when I turned out. As I was changing, a whole list of things that previously had never entered my head before a game kept popping out as 'Oh, I need to check that' – like a burgeoning shopping list as you push a trolley around Sainsbury's.

When a player is thrown his shirt it probably doesn't register as anything at all, but my first real problem was what to do about both teams turning up to play in red and white. With neither side wanting to change their traditional strip and bearing in mind something had to be done to make the game start, we ended up with both captains accepting my offer to do the best I could to differentiate between them, but that any cases of mistaken identity would have to be accepted with good grace. In the end, as if by magic, fifteen blue shirts were conjured up and this headache went away.

It is this authority and indeed duty to manage the whole affair that brings a referee both pressure but also pleasure; which of us does not harbour some small leaning towards occasional dictatorship, even if benevolent? This must be the principal attraction for any person who takes to the dark side, as it is known in rugby circles. While many might deny this seduction, it has to be so or a referee is not doing his job. OK, they are not here to watch you, but if you don't exert an authority and thereby a significant influence, the game will not function properly and whatever spectacle they might have come to watch will not happen either.

Even though my former playing days hit the heights, I still felt uncomfortable going into each changing room and laying down the law on the laws; what I would and would not tolerate. I was remembering what I used to think when on the other end of these lectures. I used to make up my mind in about fifteen seconds as to what a particular referee was going to be like from what he said at this juncture. Too familiar meant inappropriately lax; too officious meant that the bloke undoubtedly knew every law and at some point would demonstrate this by blowing continually and signalling in an overtly precise fashion – and

God help the referee who turned up with brand-new white bootlaces.

As it was, my reputation for being somewhat pathological about the scrum had already infiltrated the minds of the respective front rows and scrum-halves who volunteered to put the ball in straight and not to push early.

With regard to the general stuff, all I felt I needed to stress was the tackle, which I addressed by saying, 'The main thing I want in the tackle is for the tackler to fuck off straight away. And I mean instantly, not quickly.'

I didn't feel the need to warn about backchat because the sanctions are there to deal with that and, anyway, a referee who says this first betrays an insecurity that is recognised by players as soon as he opens his mouth.

If a captain is clever he will use this to his advantage by pressuring a referee with gentle suggestions which, although seemingly inoffensive and indeed helpful, will be regular and will contrast to the open challenges the referee might receive from the opposition. 'Is the gap [in the line-out] OK, ref?' 'Are we ten?' 'Are you happy with our binding?' These are ways of highlighting that you are doing it right and by implication they are not. In this way a subconscious store of goodwill accrues which can come out in the way that the 50/50 decisions are made.

As the teams lined up for the kick-off I checked both captains were ready and with a frisson of excitement blew the whistle. What followed was, by common assent, a flawless demonstration of officiating. I made no mistakes, and the players, other officials and crowd had nothing to complain about – as a referee you cannot realistically expect positive acclamation. The game flowed and Park scored a scintillating try with the sort of handling that unfortunately escapes England's backs all too often.

Yes, for the two and a half minutes I was on the field I was brilliant; until my right calf tore and it felt like I had been shot by some embittered and jealous member of the fraternity, envious at all the misplaced attention my foray to the dark side had attracted. I could only hobble off with laughter ringing in my ears; my embarrassment complete and pride demolished.

Lessons I perhaps didn't learn: nobody likes a smart-arse, and get fit before you do this.

Cynics on a slippery slope at Winter Olympics 2010 in Vancouver

February 2010

Four years ago the silver medal won by Shelley Rudman in the skeleton was not given the respect it deserved in some quarters, including the sports media, who should have known better. Sliding on a tea tray, glorified tobogganing and the like were the sort of dismissive comments that ignored or failed to understand the courage and athleticism needed to achieve that feat.

The death of Georgian Nodar Kumaritashvili on the ultra-fast and treacherous Whistler course should not have been necessary for the athletes taking part in the Winter Olympic sliding events to be given the esteem they deserve.

Anyone thinking beyond the stupid cliché should be able to understand that the G forces generated by hurtling down the ice at 90mph require the competitor to have tremendous musculature to maintain a rigid position.

The ability then to make minute adjustments to take the best line into and out of multiple bends takes not only physical prowess but the ability to sustain intense concentration at high stress levels, with reaction times measured in tenths of a second.

Whatever the outcome of the challenge from Britain's athletes, let us hear no more of the rubbish parroted by the indolent and ignorant.

Danny Cipriani – it is the man
he needs to sort out

February 2010

See, I told you something was not quite right with the Danny Cipriani situation, and, sure enough, the occasionally wayward but occasionally sublime talent is to ply his trade in the expanded Super 15 tournament, for the ironically aptly named Melbourne Rebels.

In sporting terms the Cipriani case demonstrates most facets of an increasing inability to take anything approaching a balanced view about populist topics, which is one of the less attractive and least helpful developments in the British psyche.

His self-imposed exile has led to polarised reactions from the rugby world. These range from claims that Cipriani has been run out of town as a result of unsympathetic management at club and international level, to personal criticism of the player as a mere playboy without wit or character; oh and by the way, he has always been overrated.

The truth is that there is fault all round and its roots were sown a long time ago. Cipriani's advisers have not helped him with their positioning of him as a fashion-celebrity marketing vehicle before he established his sporting credentials. The natural excitement of fame, exacerbated by a photogenic partner, has not been tempered by hard advice. Add to this Cipriani's lack of worldly experience and you have the ingredients for a Shakespearean tragedy.

There are many readers who will have greeted the revelation that Cipriani sought counselling over his depressed state as merely confirmation of him as another weak-willed youth. They will dismiss Cipriani as someone who is unable to exhibit the necessary fortitude, a product of an indulgent society. And while doing so they will probably make some allusion to our troops in the Second World War or Afghanistan. In doing so, they will display not only their lack of pity but also miss the point: is it not wrong that a player is placed in a position where he feels he has to seek such advice?

On the other side of this issue there is a case to answer by those who have irresponsibly trumpeted Cipriani's talents before they proved to be long-standing. Some of this has been the penchant for pushing the news agenda. Yet there has also been a complete lack of understanding over what was really being recommended for Cipriani, and the stage at which it was proposed that he effectively take control of the destiny of England's attacking options for the immediate future.

It is cruel to overburden a young player with your hopes and unfulfilled desires because few sportsmen can cope with such a burden. Moreover, England's inability to sustain a coherent attacking strategy is a conundrum of epic proportions and is not the responsibility of Cipriani; nor is it capable of being solved by him alone.

I think I was wrong in asserting that England could not afford to lose such a talent because it now seems to me that the best option for all is for him to get on with his life elsewhere, with the strict caveat that he avoids the attentions of the media in his new environment. Go and play, come back a better, wiser player; because though it seems like a lifetime, you will still be only twenty-seven by the time the World Cup comes to England, and five or six years of good rugby either side of that competition would be more than most achieve. Above all, sort yourself out as a man and the rest will take care of itself.

A view from the cheap seats

February 2010

If anyone involved with the team still does not understand that there is serious disillusionment about the performance of England, they could do worse than take a couple of hours to talk to people from the grass roots of rugby. They are, by the way, the vast majority of the English game, which too often is seen as only the upper televised echelon, and they are withering in their assessment of recent performances and more particularly the excuses and assessments given on camera by the England captain and management alike.

A welcome correction to my rugby focus last weekend came in the guise of a visit to Halifax RUFC, a club who tried to pursue the professional path, only to fail, as many others have, but a club who survived, unlike many others, to face a difficult yet sustainable future without debt.

They know rugby in those parts and their simple and direct criticisms were as accurate as they were scathing. They know England are not world-beaters at the moment, but, as one seasoned player put it, they are sick of seven years of being told England are a side in transition, particularly as they cannot see into what it is intended they transform. He ended by saying that he could not bring himself to watch the last match; and that is something about which England should express regret.

Shambles in British tennis is too big for Tim Henman to solve

March 2010

If Tim Henman takes up the post which will be vacant, sooner or later, of captain to the Great Britain Davis Cup tennis team, not only does he need his head examining, so do the people who believe he should be offered the role.

It cannot be disputed that British tennis, Andy Murray and Laura Robson excepted, is a shambles, and an expensive one at that. What is contentious is who is responsible and how best to get out of the present predicament, which is now eliciting sympathy rather than sniggering; yes, it is so bad we are now being pitied.

Calls for the head of Roger Draper, the chief executive of the Lawn Tennis Association, are backed by the disastrous decline of the British team in the world rankings to somewhere level with the Galápagos Islands. That Draper has failed to arrest this decline is not surprising given that a while ago he appeared not to know to which long-term plan he was working and by what criteria he was to be judged. Nevertheless, Draper was given a five-year contract extension till 2013 and his removal would be expensive. If and when he does go, on whatever terms, the people responsible for this foolhardy deal should also go.

Draper may have installed a better regime at the elite level of tennis and this is necessary when you get the raw talent to work with, but without a regular supply of such talent all that you get is expensively treated also-rans; which is the case at the moment.

The calls for Henman or Greg Rusedski to take charge are misguided; what coaching/management experience do they have? The latter has some but is not, shall we say, universally popular in tennis circles; the former was a great player, but as English rugby is finding out there is no automatic translation from world-class player to world-class coach/manager.

Those who argue for Murray to have a say in the appointment are similarly foolish. Why would the Scot want to get embroiled in this farce anyway, when he has more than enough to do trying to win trophies? What does he know about the wider administrative and management role of a chief executive? Additionally, the deference shown in giving Murray a say would create a bad precedent; similar largesse towards John Terry at Chelsea has shown that, once bestowed, this sort of elevation sets a player apart and makes him disproportionately powerful.

If you want to look to the Murray family for guidance the best person to ask is the formidable Judy, who had the foresight to remove herself and her son from the clutches of the LTA and who has already gone through the process of planning all-inclusive tennis facilities.

It actually matters not who takes over from John Lloyd because they will face a problem which will take years and radical action to alleviate. The one thing that nobody has raised is the image of tennis in Britain as middle-class, snooty and elite (in the wrong way). The attitude of the tennis establishment mirrors that of a former commercial director of the Royal Opera House. When asked about the elitist image of opera he simply said that he didn't agree opera was elitist; when you are so far in denial there is little chance that things will change.

The history of the way in which tennis was established in Britain shows the class system dominated its early development and – through privately owned and run clubs – still exerts its baleful influence. The LTA is run by the same sort of people and its initiatives go via the committees of these clubs who have little incentive to change; turkeys and Christmas and all that. This might not be a problem if tennis emulated rowing and regularly produced athletes of world standing, but it palpably does not.

The only way to get the right talent is to widen the playing base and get children playing at the earliest age possible. To do this would mean taking the contentious decision to force LTA member clubs to have minimum percentages of members in categories like age, sex and ethnicity.

It means mandating links with local schools – state and private – and guaranteeing court time for school kids and their families. A signal of intent would be to allow the public to use the LTA courts in Roehampton when they are not used by elite players. Another push along this road would be a caveat that any Government funding would only go to clubs that had such criteria in place.

Unfortunately, even if the LTA was able to persuade or compel its membership to instigate such systems, it can do little to influence the club from which the rest of tennis takes its lead – the All England Lawn Tennis and Croquet Club. This is the most elite club in Britain and one which delights in this status.

If tennis wants Henman to help it should ask him to use his position on the management committee of the All England Club to get that institution to open its doors to the public. There could be no more powerful signal of intent and inclusiveness than the All England Club announcing that, save for the major courts, the remainder of its facilities could be used by anyone.

The fantastic experience of playing at Wimbledon would attract year-round queues similar to those during Wimbledon fortnight and the powerful message sent out could not be achieved by spending any amount of money on advertising, marketing campaigns and local initiatives.

That this suggestion will provoke indignation and spluttering around the breakfast tables of Britain's tennis establishment merely shows how entrenched is this elitism.

OK, in a free society it is right that your club, as a private concern, can have who it wants as a member, but don't then bleat about how this plays out at a national level and don't pretend you are not part of the problem.

79

We're mad as hell and we're not going to take this any more – England Six Nations nightmare

March 2010

Can any of the England team, management or players answer the following questions: in which 1976 film did Peter Finch win an Oscar for Best Actor for his portrayal of the news anchor Howard Beale, who threatens to commit suicide on air to increase his show's declining TV ratings, and what was his signature catchphrase that was taken up by disaffected viewers? The answers are *Network* and 'We're mad as hell and we're not going to take this any more.'

The England team, both managers and players, are on the verge of creating a legion of fans who shortly will be following Beale's disaffected viewers and yelling something similar at Twickenham.

Further, their inability to front up and admit there are serious deficiencies to their game in public makes them appear like the film's Best Actress-winning Faye Dunaway, to whom the following description was applied to her character Diana by Max Schumacher (William Holden): 'indifferent to suffering, insensitive to joy. All of life is reduced to the common rubble of banality.'

When the England team bus had difficulty getting past security into Murrayfield stadium perhaps we should have predicted what was to come. Then again, the darkest dreams of thousands of desperately optimistic travelling supporters could not have included eighty minutes during which their heroes would not be able to unlock the Scotland defence barring accident or gift.

As a nation not traditionally noted for largesse, the Scots saved their opponents' face by generously extending a habit which is maddeningly frustrating for their supporters – not scoring tries, despite plentiful possession and promising approach play. Yet at least they can see a pattern, some promise, some passion. If you are English you are not given that modicum of comfort.

There is little to be gained from listing England's technical and constitutional flaws because they remain the same and have been pointed out before. However, you have to add to this a number of issues which, while being part of the background, are nevertheless contributing to fans feeling alternately suicidal or homicidal.

The slothful manner in which the forwards get set for scrums and line-outs adds to the general torpor and lack of dynamism because it betrays a lack of mental rigour, from which speed of deed is virtually impossible.

If it is difficult to read this column without it sounding like a hackneyed whinge, it is because the same faults go unaddressed either by selection or game plan. If we keep going on about it, it is because it keeps going on.

The narrow focus of winning justifies the means, any means, but it only works if you do, in fact, win and no amount of talk at being disappointed that we didn't put it away, were a shade unlucky or the referee was a **** will help.

The England players and management may think that this is another in a welter of unjustified and ignorant criticism, but they are right on the edge of losing whatever support they had from past achievements. Martin Johnson, the England manager, may not care, but his personal store of goodwill is similarly scant. He should care because behind any withdrawal of benevolence there is justification and, with a hostile audience, an already difficult job may prove impossible.

Johnson remains determined to see the positives, but the reality is that there was only one: they didn't lose against a team who score in threes. England could not even fashion the right field position to give Toby Flood a decent chance to kick the winning dropped goal. If any England player reads this and bridles at the unfairness of it all, he needs to grow up. Though you are not paid like footballers, you do receive half the national average annual wage per game. If you think this is another bitter rant you need to spend some time with supporters who are tired of hearing you talk a good game but see you fail to deliver.

All of which neatly leads us back to the world of celebrity, fantasy and entertainment. As a team, England may crave the flattery and attention that accompanies international status, but they have to bear the inseparable burden of fulfilling supporters' expectations by winning consistently; if they cannot do this they have to entertain. Presently they do neither, which is a plot no creative director would countenance. Fans are now pleading to be given one thing or the other and are so desperate that they do not care which.

Meanwhile, in the Night Garden, the land of the consensually deluded, everybody's asleep. Upsey Daisy; Macca Pacca; the Tombliboos; but wait, somebody's not in bed – it is Captain Iggle Piggle Borthwick, wandering alone in an amazing world, trying to rouse himself from his own soporific oratory. If only it was a cartoon dream.

80

Another one bites the dust – the Watmore resignation

March 2010

It would make a good sitcom: full of characters, from the meek to the mean, and everything in between, with the added glamour of not only footballers but their wives as well, all resplendent with fantastic amounts of cash. This is the ongoing battle for control of football in England, a grisly soap opera that would be an entertaining diversion from real life if the issues involved were not so serious and the stakes so high.

You don't need to know the identity of an organisation or its sphere of operation to know that when it has six chief executives in just over ten years it has deep-seated flaws. The departure of Ian Watmore, only the latest of the indecently short engagements, has provoked an array of opinions from commentators. Many refuse to articulate what they know to be the case – even though it is obvious to people not at the incestuous heart of the footballing world – namely, that it is the professional game via its equal representation on the FA Board that is the root of these serial failures.

The apex of the English game is run by the canniest of operators in the guise of Richard Scudamore. A more efficient operator it is difficult to identify and his disarming manner merely cloaks a laser-like focus on the interests of his organisation. So successful has he been that the professional game has been able to disavow responsibility for multiple failures by the FA when it has as much responsibility for these as the amateur bodies that have the other half of the votes at Board level.

My colleague Henry Winter knows more than most about football in England, yet even his take on this saga evidences the way in which the focus on these matters is invariably skewed away from those responsible. His call for real leaders at the FA runs smack into the fact that anyone truly of that ilk, with an agenda for reclaiming power from football's professional interests and trying to wrest the top end of the game away from potentially ruinous debt levels, will suffer the same fate as Watmore and his predecessors.

Recent discussions of the manner in which Watmore attempted to revitalise the FA Cup included a claim that the FA required a real general to lead it into battle against the combined forces of the Premier League, Champions League and Carling Cup. However, if this were transposed into the setting of the last world war, it would be like half of Churchill's War Cabinet also being members of the German High Command. Not even the man voted the Greatest Briton could succeed in those circumstances.

It is said that the following are far stronger chief executives: the Professional Footballers' Association's Gordon Taylor, the League Managers' Association's Richard Bevan and the Premier League's Richard Scudamore. How can they not be when they are constitutionally able to destabilise their opponent in any face-off?

The language used to describe Watmore has been little short of insulting. His dismissal as little more than a civil servant or a suit overlooks his twenty-four-year career with Accenture PLC, a global management consulting, technology services and outsourcing company, of which he became managing director. Figures from ADVFN (a leading online financial information site) for 2009 list Accenture as having a $30 billion market capitalisation, a Gross Profit Margin of 32.2 per cent and a Total Debt/Equity (Gearing Ratio) of 0 per cent. Coming from that sort

of business background, it is no wonder Watmore found it difficult to come to terms with footballing economics.

Watmore went after attempting to instigate reforms on the regulation and financial accountability for the clubs. Attempts by the
FA to deny his proposals were being thwarted came with a statement that stated, 'Further to reports following Ian Watmore's
announcement, the Board are clear that the professional game [the
clubs] has not blocked proposals for change.' This is the same
Board, half of which is made up of the very people accused of the
blocking. It is not surprising that it continued to say, 'Additionally,
the Board does not accept that Ian's departure is down to any one
individual or any personality clash with Ian.' This tacitly leaves
open the possibility/probability that all the professional game's
Board members were against him.

Lord Mawhinney and David Davies have both named the FA's
inherent instability as the cause of this latest departure but they
have stopped short of what needs to be said: namely that you
cannot have an effective governing and disciplinary body, one
which also runs the national team, which has an effective veto
granted to one constituent part. Its and their interests will always
differ and even when some communality does occur, the priorities of the two factions may differ. No one will come out and say
that the representation and thereby influence of the professional
game has to be reduced for the FA to have any chance of working properly. The club v. country debate almost always takes place
at the levels of selection, player release, insurance and so on; the
consequences of this schism go much deeper and it is at that fundamental level that the debate over change has to start.

French Rugby Federation's programme gesture was magnificent

March 2010

I didn't take much notice of the programmes given to me before the latest France v. England rugby union game; I always have a programme to refer to.

What I didn't know was that no members of the public had the same because of the decision of the French Rugby Federation to withdraw the programme because an article made reference to an incident in 2001 involving Riki Flutey.

If, as I am satisfied is the case, this was not done for legal reasons, then it was a magnificent gesture by the French in acting on and not just talking about the right to privacy of an individual. Given the loss of revenue you cannot imagine this being matched by many other organisations.

Cruel and unusual – the bleep test

March 2010

It is a simple test. Two lines, twenty metres apart. You walk/jog to the far line and turn when the short bleep sounds, and do the same again and again and again.

You carry on doing this as the bleeps get faster until you fall over exhausted. At first it seems ludicrously easy, but soon it gets harder, and at one point you feel as though your lungs will burst and you start to get light-headed. Until you know better, you think that you cannot run any more; but the truth is that this is the signal that oxygen death is approaching and, with the right will, you can probably go for another minute or so before your body finally seizes up and you literally cannot run another step.

This is the 'bleep test' that the Government's chief medical officer, Sir Liam Donaldson, wants to make every schoolchild do as a regular measure of their fitness. It is a great idea, in theory, because it is simple, consistent and, if you don't allow cheating (any of the England squad of my generation will tell you how – for a small fee), a reliable way of measuring increases and decreases in aerobic fitness, which is the only one that matters for general living.

Painful memories of this test bring to mind the words cruel and unusual, and let there be no doubt that if you are not fit it is purgatory at best. It is also certain that on its first administration there will be a number of kids who faint, vomit or involuntarily evacuate themselves; or all three. At that point you can see the pencils being sharpened for personal injury claims and though this point has an element of levity, therein lies one of the basic problems: should you force children to do something that is good for them in the long run, but in their present indolent and obese state could well be uncomfortable and in a very small number of cases injurious to short-term health?

Unfortunately those who rightly take the Government to task for many of its unnecessary 'nanny-state' initiatives have included this proposal as an example without thinking things through. We do not apply a hands-off approach to any other subject taught in our schools; there is no reason why physical education should not be treated in the same way as the rest of the curriculum. In fact, it is illogical not to do this and it is a wonder that this anomaly has been left unaddressed for so long. You would never invest huge sums of money and time on a subject without measuring what success it brings. To demonstrate how aberrant is the present state of affairs ask yourself this: would you accept that your child attending two hours' science lessons a week was sufficient to assume he or she had achieved the appropriate standard without there being some form of nationally consistent test to prove this?

There are always claims that such tests lead to stigmatisation of fat children, but they are fat whether or not they are tested and it is hardly likely that the taunts would be modified to include the extra jibe that 'You fell 3 per cent on your bleep test.' Actually, the victims may find comfort in being able to say, at least to themselves, that they know they have made progress because of the fact that their scores get better. They will see improvements in the figures to encourage their efforts long before they see a waif-like figure in the mirror.

I suspect that quite a lot of the indignation about this proposal is vicarious and comes from similarly obese parents who will not change their lifestyle, and by example are harming their children, unwittingly in some cases but not in the majority. Added to this, there are those chronically prejudiced against sport and those prepared to criticise any attempt to coerce activity out of lazy children, while simultaneously remaining rabidly dogmatic about the need for children to be inculcated with Latin and history.

When you consider the precedents set during our schooldays in all manner of areas, should we not accept that there is not only a responsibility to make children learn about fitness, whether they want to or not, but also an acceptance that it is for their and our general and long-term benefit? The tests should go further and include cholesterol levels which take seconds but which are reliable indicators of which children may have problems later in life if they do not amend their diet and lifestyle. We test and vaccinate for many things; why is this so different?

If the Government was really serious about making this a long-term measure and a standard test which would become part of the curriculum, it should have our wholehearted support. Unfortunately, there have been so many other off-the-top-of-the-head, headline-grabbing stunts that had no chance of being implemented that you have no way of knowing how serious the Government's intent is. If we are accused by those in power of being unduly cynical about this important subject then it is their fault because even those of us who are passionate about sport and the many benefits it offers have been here many times before.

The *Daily Telegraph* School Sports Awards have the tangential benefit of allowing us to get unadulterated information as to the current state of school sport and playing fields which have been and are still being sold during this Government's tenure, despite express guarantees to the contrary. The promise and claim of a minimum of two hours' sport each week have been distorted and ignore the fact that travel and changing times severely lessen the time spend doing sport for many kids. For some it is in reality as low as forty minutes.

So, if you are serious, bring this test in as part of a range of tests. Make them compulsory, and for once do no listen to focus groups, civil servants or anyone who cannot fit on a Disneyland ride.

83

We won't get fooled again

March 2010

'Change it had to come, We knew it all along . . . But the world looks just the same, And history ain't changed . . . Meet the new boss, Same as the old boss.' As Rob Andrew pens his report on the England team's performance this season he should power out the classic track 'Won't Get Fooled Again' by The Who; it should remind him of the mood of the rugby public.

Against a background of solid scepticism Andrew will have to do a job of truly epic proportions to convince a doubting audience that Martin Johnson is firmly on track to improve English rugby and fulfil his own cheery goal of sustained success at the top of world rugby. And if he thinks one creditable losing performance against the French in their final Six Nations match will obscure hours of unconvincing and unimaginative play, he had better bring a flak jacket with him when he releases the report.

Just so we don't allow the goalposts to be moved (perish the thought), Johnson took over from Brian Ashton, who had a 54.5 per cent success rate, his team were runners-up in the last World Cup and second in that season's Six Nations, the final game of which saw a 33–10 gubbing of Ireland featuring someone called Danny Cipriani. Remember him?

Johnson's ratio of wins to date stands at 42.1 per cent, but if you include the 2008 New Zealand tour, when he was appointed but did not travel, it is 38.09 per cent, below that of Andy

Robinson, Ashton's predecessor, at 40.9 per cent. Moreover, while England played well against France, in terms of portents the aforementioned game when England thrashed Ireland promised more and it didn't save Ashton.

Whenever you get close to feeling sorry for Andrew, think about his pay packet, which always does the trick. His position at the Rugby Football Union as director of elite rugby is highly rewarded and should demand commensurate results. It is irrelevant whether the incumbent is giving it his all: we are entitled to say show us your titles.

One of Andrew's main problems will be trying to disassociate whatever effect he has had on the performance of the international structure, given that it appears he has, unwisely, been involved in certain managerial functions – another structural fault in the system. Hands up those who think he will recommend radical, or indeed any, change? Thought so. No, it will be steady as she goes, just like two similar reviews into Ashton's tenure, and it is from his conclusions to those reports that he may look to counter recent criticism of his own performance.

What many have forgotten is that Andrew recommended retaining Ashton, not appointing Johnson. Further, Johnson was given absolute discretion on which of the coaches were retained – all of them, as it turned out. This fact allows Andrew, with a lot of justification, to disavow responsibility for the present unsatisfactory position. However, Andrew must be at least partially culpable from this review onwards, because he now has the opportunity to recommend Johnson's removal.

What we all should now remember is who mandated that Andrew appoint Johnson: the management committee, chaired by Martyn Thomas. It was Thomas who was forced to confirm when Andrew was engaged that his committee retained final jurisdiction over appointments. He transparently did not recognise the inherent irony in his use of the following words: 'We'd be pretty foolish to appoint Rob and then ignore his recommendations.'

Should the Johnson experiment ultimately fail, Thomas should pay the price along with anyone else who gets the boot. Hands up all those who think this will happen? Thought so. If, as is likely, Johnson stays, there remains the conundrum of who is responsible for the assessment of the other coaches: Johnson or Andrew? If it is the former you have the unqualified and inexperienced evaluating the experienced. If the latter, what does that say of Johnson's promised autonomy? If, as may be the case, it is a bit of both, you have the worst of all worlds because *in extremis* they can both point at the other.

Whatever is said publicly, there has at least been superficial consideration of replacing Johnson, but we are now so close to the 2011 World Cup that, as with Ashton's appointment in December 2006, any change would probably not dramatically improve England's chances. It is doubtful whether a top-class replacement would step in. Any candidate would have to doubt whether he had sufficient time to succeed. On top of this I would counsel them to consider too how this same management board treated Ashton.

If bringing this up again angers the RFU, I would merely point out that nobody forced them to handle Ashton's removal in such a disgraceful, and probably illegal, manner, and if they think that went unnoticed, well, that would be pretty foolish.

84

Polo-lite is just the kind of horseplay I can enjoy

April 2010

The following tale is probably the sum total of my experience with horses, other than watching the odd race meeting and visiting the Cartier International Polo Tournament as a hanger-on.

While in Argentina the England rugby squad were invited, en masse, to an afternoon's relaxation in the form of a horse trek to the summit of one of the nearby peaks, from which, we were assured, the views were splendid. We were given our mounts and some rudimentary instructions on how to stay on the horse and what to do if things got out of hand.

Armed with dangerously little knowledge we set off, though it has to be said it was with vastly differing degrees of enthusiasm. It wasn't too taxing, given that it mainly involved little more than the odd canter, only a few steep inclines and the fauna on the way to the top was interesting.

We reached the summit in about twenty minutes and the views were indeed magnificent, although one of the forwards claimed he couldn't see them because of all the mountains in the way. However, the unanimous verdict afterwards was that it had been a journey worth taking.

Sorry, correct that: there was a lone dissenting voice; that of the then youthful prop from Barking, Jason Leonard. For as we mounted up to return down whence we had come Mr Leonard appeared on the pathway dragging his reluctant mount behind him, exclaiming in his broad east London brogue, 'The fucking thing refused to go more than twenty yards, I've had to pull it all the way up.' Depending on your view, the horse was either unconscionably lazy or extremely wise, having declined to carry 19 stone up the hillside for no apparent reward.

You see, some people have horses in their blood; not Jason obviously, but riders wax lyrical about the symbiotic relationship they have with their steeds. I have to say my enthusiasm didn't extend much further than Jason's. My ambiguous feelings about attending the Cartier event were set out in an earlier column. I hated the ambience but was enthralled by the play.

So you can imagine the lukewarm feelings I had in accepting a challenge/invitation to attend at Hurlingham Park on Wednesday, where Jodie and Jack Kidd and other world-renowned English polo players such as Kirsty Craig were launching what was termed the New Twenty20 World Series – 'Polo in the Park'.

Moreover, I was told that they, as with many other sports, were launching a simplified version of the full sport, played on a smaller field in an attempt to make polo more accessible and attractive to TV. By instinct I do not really like truncated versions of most sports but decided to find out a bit more before condemning this initiative out of hand.

In conjunction with Hammersmith and Fulham council, a group of schoolchildren from backgrounds not traditionally associated with polo had been picked to have a thirty-minute lesson in the basics of the sport. As my experience was little better than theirs, it didn't seem untoward that I take part in the same exercise.

It seems obvious, but the first thing that went through my mind as I mounted my horse was that I was relying on another animate object to achieve my goal. It is vastly different from riding a motorcycle, which you can chuck into corners knowing that if you have got your bit right, it will go where it is supposed to.

Horses have a mind of their own and my horse was probably thinking, 'Who is this lard-arse?', also recognising a novice rider as soon as I fidgeted about in the saddle. Trusting your wellbeing to something with an independent mind is not the easiest of concepts when you have been used to being in control of what you do and when you do it, but this is the reason riders say after the event 'I'm so pleased for the horse.'

There is a sodality about anything that is achieved in which vicarious enjoyment supplements the individual, and, because the basic elements of trust and loyalty have been tested, the accomplishment feels more special. My aim was to stay on the horse and maybe hit a few balls. However, when I started to get involved with the technical aspects I became increasingly fascinated and determined to get things right.

When I managed not to pull up my horse just as I was about to swing, I made quite a few satisfying shots, but as usual my impetuosity demanded that I try to go faster and hit harder, with the result that I was less effective. The one time I did nearly come to grief the blow to my private parts was a sufficient reminder not to get too cocky (so to speak).

On Friday 4–6 June inclusive, the World Polo Series will be held at Hurlingham Park and I will now be a willing attendee. A shortened version of polo does not threaten or alter the basic skills, unlike what happens when some sports are shortened, and the physicality will be heightened by the reduction of space. Like in all things, the experts will make a difficult skill appear mundane but it will be a world away from the foppish celebrity of Windsor, something anyone can enjoy.

Polo cannot get away from the fact that you have to have a bit of money to take part, but the demographic of the players varies far more than expected. One of my best friends, a Brentwood RFC third XV player, semi-professional cage fighter and all-round lunatic, plays with his equally humble mates in Ham.

Further, the real expense comes with wanting to own your own horse.

Many people now hire the horses and it is possible to turn up at some clubs and play for the afternoon for only £30. Down the Fulham Road at Stamford Bridge you will be pushed to find a seat at that price and it certainly won't get you a ticket at Twickenham.

85

Tiger Woods can now do no right for some critics

April 2010

It is apparent that some journalists will kick Tiger Woods whatever he does or says: the coverage of last week's Masters demonstrated this fully. Woods's admirably frank pre-tournament press conference was dismissed in various ways. It was said that he rehearsed his answers. Of course he did, and so would you if you knew that any small inconsistency would be seized upon. He was criticised for using psychobabble and the language of the counselled. Well, that is what happens when you examine your psyche.

Forcing yourself to do this is not a cheap option and anyone who says so without having done so is an ignorant fool. Moreover, what is he supposed to use by way of reply when a question directly addresses psychological issues?

You see, Woods is damned whatever he does because if from this point he shows contrition and tries to atone through good works it will be said that he is merely trying to curry favour and buy his way back into our affections.

If he focuses just on golf and ignores any wider enquiries he will be labelled cold, aloof and arrogant.

His finishing position of fourth was remarkable given his five-month absence from the game. But even this was trashed by some commentators, likewise the achievement of winner Phil Mickelson was cheapened by unnecessary juxtaposing of anything he did with Woods – his demeanour, past private life and so on were all mentioned. None was relevant to the matter at hand.

86

David Beckham has an important role to play for England

April 2010

In spite of his unavailability through injury, David Beckham could still turn out to be one of the linchpins in England's attempt to win the World Cup in South Africa which starts in just fifty days. While Beckham's torn Achilles tendon has taken away the midfielder's ability to deliver wicked balls into the box, it has also removed the perennial debate about his form and whether he justifies inclusion as a starter or substitute. It has also given Fabio Capello the perfect non-playing captain for the tournament.

Capello's announcement that Beckham has accepted his offer to augment England's management team in South Africa has received a mixed reception. Some have labelled it a PR stunt and others have carped that this is a sinecure and has been done more for England's 2018 World Cup bid than the imminent competition.

If Capello is wise – and every indication thus far is that he is – he will give Beckham a wide-ranging role and one of substance. Although international teams are not familiar with it, many club teams recognise the position of club captain and Beckham's role should be substantially the same.

A supporting role will be a test of Beckham's selflessness, but at least he is in the position of knowing he cannot play so will not have at the back of his mind the natural instinct of a competitor, which usually manifests itself in wanting your team to do well but your direct rival for the position to play badly.

What Beckham can impart by way of footballing nous and technique is not difficult to define: delivery of the ball into the box at pace is going to be an important issue, particularly with a strike force led by Wayne Rooney, who, although much improved in the air, is not a giant. However, it is with indefinable things that Beckham's experience may prove more valuable. Each World Cup tournament is by its nature unique but there are common threads. The pattern of group stage followed by knock-out is familiar but not in the claustrophobic atmosphere of a team headquarters, itself situated in one country which for one month will have nothing on its mind but football.

The build-up to games will by now have been set and the management should know the schedule and content of the preparation. However, what is equally, if not more important, is the downtime, of which there is plenty.

The overall psyche of a squad is something that can be affected by seemingly small things, which often have nothing to do with what has taken place during games. Of these the relationship with the public, and in this I include the media, is one which can enhance or destabilise a squad. During the six weeks the squad are together they will have untold demands and requests for players to be available for interviews, to meet dignitaries, sponsors, Uncle Tom Cobley and all. Players know they have to do this but in reality do not want to go through what will undoubtedly be the same raft of questions, each time phrased slightly differently, but essentially amounting to the same point – how do you think you will do/are doing? Beckham is easily capable of fielding any questions in the right way and by removing a substantial amount of this sort of work he will receive the untold thanks of the squad.

Hardly any player looks forward to doing a glad-handing

session and not just for the reason suspected by most of the public: that they think they are above such things. Many are uncomfortable speaking in public and earning vast sums of money just means players have to go through with interviews, but the unease is not removed. Some are rightly aware that certain journalists do not have their best interests at heart and have been sent not to report on football but to find scandal that can adorn a front page.

In addition are the regular periods of two or three hours during which there is insufficient time to do anything substantial but sufficient time to become thoroughly bored. There may be some truth in the maxim that only boring people get bored, but footballers are used to having their regimes dictated by others or else being in comfortable home surroundings.

The World Cup will not match many of the player's expectations of one of the premier sporting events. They will see little of the beauty of the host country, but a lot of the inside of airports and coaches. They will experience little of the culture, but will become familiar with every inch of their training camp and the inside of a hotel, even one that is palatial and has first-class facilities, can soon become dull and oppressive. Many of the options open to people on their holidays are not going to be there for players; even the mundane stroll around the shops is not going to be available because of the hordes of media and public.

Beckham can forewarn players who have only an inkling of how limiting this feels and that they will, for most of the time, not feel part of what for everyone else is a glorious and riotous sojourn. This may sound ridiculous but one of the more memorable things for me in the 1995 Rugby World Cup, also in South Africa, were the team quizzes held among the England players.

And as an afterthought, as Beckham's dead-ball skills are legendary, he could use his experience to convince his fellow squad members that they should practise these with a religious fervour and not as reluctant schoolboys. I would get each prospective penalty-taker to put £50,000 in the pot and hold shootouts after each training session – the winner at the end of the tournament takes all. If Beckham can help to end England's dreadful record regarding penalties he will have done more than he ever could on the pitch.

87

Any political party that prioritises sport would get my vote – but there isn't one

April 2010

Sport occupies an enormous slice of media attention compared to its direct contribution to the UK economy, but it also provides huge benefits to the country – and considerably more than its siblings, culture and media. At its best, sport also effectively backs up many Government departments in their initiatives on key issues such as childhood obesity, antisocial behaviour and the decline of respect in society.

As sport is also the only activity where partaking and succeeding does not depend on your wealth, connections or race, you would think it would have a high priority with all parties.

Add to this the position sport plays in the voters' psyche and the vicarious popularity a sporting success brings a government and you would expect politicians to recognise the unique position of sport; but, no, it remains lumped with the others in Whitehall, fighting for every inch of territory.

A look at the party election manifestos shows how much regard the politicians really have for sport.

The Labour manifesto is 78 pages long, and out of 30,755 words there were 550 dealing with sport: 1.8 per cent. The Conservative Party equivalent is 131 pages in total, containing 28,850 words of which are 123 words on sport: 0.43 per cent. The

Liberal Democrats' manifesto has 21,600 words, with 96 words on sport: 0.44 per cent.

The Labour document, at Chapter Seven, focuses heavily on the 2012 Olympic Games in London, pledging, 'We will ensure that the Olympics are delivered on time and on budget, to the highest standards. Britain will be the first Olympic hosts to create a world-class sports system, from elite level to the grass-roots.'

Labour also promises to bring 'mutualism to the heart of football' and promises that: 'Sports governing bodies will be empowered to scrutinise takeovers of clubs, ensuring they are in the long-term interests of the club and the sport. We will develop proposals to enable registered Supporters Trusts to buy stakes in their club.' This falls short of a leaked earlier claim that Labour would legislate to allow fans to buy 25 per cent of clubs. In the Tory manifesto, the Conservatives promise 'to reform the governance arrangements in football to enable co-operative ownership models to be established by supporters.'

The Labour statement about creating the first world-class sports system is nonsense. The Australians produced world-class Games in 2000, and their national Institute of Sport was delivering world-class athletes and coaches twenty years ago and continues to do so. The pledge concerning mutualism, whatever that is, is also pointless, as is the ambiguous and noncommittal guff put out by the Tories on football governance; the Lib Dems didn't cover the subject.

This is not the view of Dave Boyle, the chief executive of Supporters Direct, who says, 'I've been reading manifesto documents for years and sport, let alone football, has never been an electoral issue before, so I'm delighted.'

The acceptance of this sort of pie-in-the-sky must be manna for party spin doctors and this is where many football supporters do not understand the overall framework of laws in the UK. The Government cannot compel a club who are constituted as a company to deal with their shares against company law. What is demanded is that shareholders are treated differently, which is expressly against the law. Unless a party is to overturn established law it cannot do anything about hostile takeovers and to pretend it can without legislating is wrong.

Moreover, the national governing bodies already have the power to regulate their sports via the membership criteria and in the case of football under rules established by the Premier League, Football League and by the Football Association for the Conference; if you don't follow the rules then you cannot play – simple.

Unfortunately the fit and proper persons test that football has established is too weak and sometimes not applied properly. This is not any politician's problem.

The Tory 'sport coverage' takes up a little more than a quarter of a page but has the pledge: 'We will deliver a successful Olympics that brings lasting benefits for the country as a whole.' Well, as all the planning has already been done, quite what they could claim credit for is a mystery.

The Liberal Democrat 'sport coverage' says they are proud that Britain is hosting the Olympic and Paralympic Games in 2012; they support bids for other high-profile events such as the 2018 World Cup 'but we believe that grass-roots sport is just as important. We will give people from all backgrounds and generations the opportunity to participate in sports.' This is simply insulting – why bother at all?

However, they do have two policies on sport: 'Use cash in dormant betting accounts to set up a capital fund for improving local sports facilities and supporting sports clubs' and they also intend to 'close loopholes that allow playing fields to be sold or built upon without going through the normal planning procedures'. Both of these are good ideas, but we have been down this route so many times before with both Tory (who started it) and Labour (who continued it) governments failing to protect sports fields. The sophistry used to justify the removal of a playing field and its replacement with a sports centre shows that it is seeking cash, not sport, where the real priority lies.

The state of the country's finances means that largesse is not a realistic hope from the next Government, but restructuring would save money and improve sport. It deserves a Cabinet seat, and a department that incorporated and housed UK Sport and Sport England in the same place would improve the often dysfunctional relationship between the Department for Culture, Media and Sport and other regulatory and funding bodies. Why do we need more than one funding body?

Any party that prioritised sport and promised to and did remove the swathes of unnecessary administration like the above and shredded large amounts of the red-tape surrounding sport might get my vote; but there isn't one.

88

Sport faces tipping point thanks to greed, scandals and incompetence

May 2010

Recently I had dinner with a close friend who used to be a sporting nut. We discussed recent sporting stories, but he then said, 'I've got to the point where I don't believe in a lot of sports. Even when I don't have doubts about what I am watching, the sideshows [by which he meant sponsors' promotions, merchandising, basically the hard sell], well, they make me feel like part of a dumb reality TV audience; patronised and exploited.'

His change in attitude had a number of causes, each contributing to his gradual move to the tipping point of disaffection. Examples of cheating were now so widespread that he wondered whether there were many sports that were pure, or at least ones where such examples were rare. When you go through the major and more popular minority sports it is difficult to find one untainted by serious allegations of malpractice: football – well, where do you start?

Right at the top, where FIFA have been at the centre of allegations of ticket fraud and corruption; rugby union – 'Bloodgate' and gouging; cricket – ball tampering and the Indian Premier League scandal; Formula One – Briatore and any given week's threat of legal proceedings over something or other; even table tennis – bat-coating to gain extra spin; all three of the main US sports have had drugs scandals; athletics; tennis – Richard

Gasquet's positive drugs test was explained away as a result of kissing a girl called Pamela; most recently, snooker has been rocked by allegations of match fixing involving John Higgins.

The above examples of recent transgressions relate to every facet of sport, from on-field to administration to disciplinary procedures. Although the focus often lands on what players do during the contest, the wider themes that relate to how a sport is run, especially when dealing with its own offenders, is equally capable of causing discontent.

It is more difficult to be categorical about why standards have slipped and some of the evidence is anecdotal, but the influence of money is unarguably one of the main factors. Substantial increases in earnings and prize money heighten the stakes, as do the increased sums wagered on events. The latter is exacerbated by changes in the nature of betting. Combined, they increase the possibilities of players and officials being corrupted by powerful operators in the betting market. While the influence of organised crime in this area goes back many years, American boxing being an example, there has been a huge increase in the complexity and worldwide nature of gambling.

An article by my colleague Simon Hart on Wednesday highlighted a recent poll suggesting that unsporting behaviour by professionals is rubbing off on the amateurs with marked increases in things like diving in football and refusing to walk in cricket.

Community sports leaders polled by the Central Council of Physical Recreation found two-thirds said on-field behaviour had degenerated over the past ten years, with cheating and arguing with officials now a common aspect of amateur sport. An overwhelming 84 per cent of those polled also believed that unfair play had increased in elite sport, with just 2 per cent saying that behaviour had improved.

Further worrying evidence of a decline in standards comes with the revelation in another report last week of a decline in people

playing eleven-a-side football and the assertion of one deputy
head of a big London comprehensive that most of his kids prefer
doing tricks with the ball as opposed to playing proper games and
that their whole approach is focused on fame and fortune.

Although there is no hard evidence for this, there is good
reason to suppose that the influence of the now seemingly
omnipresent reality and talent shows, where fame and all its
rewards are achieved in an instant, is affecting sport as much as
wider society, increasing shallowness and leading people to think
that their goals can be reached in a trice and without hard work.

Primary responsibility for shaping players' behaviour must lie
with a sport's governing body. This onus extends not just to framing workable rules and laws; it also means ensuring that best
practice is adopted in areas such as corporate governance, financial dealings, public relations and disciplinary proceedings.

A number of recent happenings have brought into disrepute a
relevant governing body and, by extension, its sport.

Witness the refusal of European Rugby Cup to answer serious
questions about its handling of 'Bloodgate', in which Harlequins'
wing Tom Williams feigned injury using fake blood capsules
against Leinster in the Heineken Cup in April 2009. There was
also the farcical prosecution of Flavio Briatore by the FIA, in
which a French court overturned the Italian's lifetime ban from
Formula One. Let's not forget FIFA's astonishing decision that
there was no legal foundation to consider Thierry Henry's handball against the Republic of Ireland because it was not a serious
infringement; or the Rugby Football Union's unconscionable
treatment of England coach Brian Ashton. All of these add to the
impression of some that sport is now an amalgam of greed and
incompetence.

However, though participants are controlled from above they
cannot escape responsibility for their actions, especially professional players. Part of this is implicit at the level at which they
perform, and part the acceptance of reward which necessarily

carries with it a duty to adhere to the regulations. That players sometimes fail in their duty cannot be avoided, but how they act thereafter is crucial. Far too often there is no personal contrition and everybody else is to blame.

The regular spin of people such as Gordon Taylor, chief executive of the Professional Footballers' Association, which excuses his members' actions rather than condemning where appropriate, only adds to the harm done to the sport.

In his address to the CCPR annual conference in London on Wednesday, Taylor spoke of many things but he identified the key word as 'respect'. If this is so, he must alter his apologist stance for players and tell it like it is. So must the League Managers' Association, which is similarly culpable when it refuses to criticise members who flout football's rules; it must refuse to sanction players when they offend and thereby set an appalling example.

You see, the problem with tipping points is that they are both unpredictable and usually irreversible.

89

Jamie Carragher's return causes far more concern than Capello Index

May 2010

In portraying Fabio Capello's link with the Capello Index as a serious matter, the footballing media are badly out of step with the average England football fan who appears more capable than seasoned watchers in placing this issue in the correct place in the scale of 'scandals', i.e. it is a minor distraction.

OK, it need not have been there at all and is surprising given Capello's previous astuteness in handling much more difficult problems, like John Terry's demotion from the England captaincy, and it has opened a small chink for hungry scandalmongers to exploit.

However, if there is no financial link it should be greeted with a shrug of the shoulders as something that would have been better not to have taken place, but in essence it is not serious, especially when set against Capello's record since he took the England manager's job.

Compare this affair to previous events that took place before past tournaments like the fallout from Glenn Hoddle's dropping of Paul Gascoigne in 1998, the multiple controversies of Sven-Göran Eriksson's reign, David Beckham's metatarsal and so on and England have been given a relatively free run in terms of negative incidents.

In any event, what does it matter about how Capello rates his players? They all know he does this every time he announces the team. Whatever way Capello assesses his players there will be room for criticism because judgement is always subjective. What should cause some concern are the thirty players Capello has had to choose for his enlarged squad and what this says about the strength of English football and England's chances of winning the World Cup.

Barring a couple of personal favourites, the vast majority of fans would agree that Capello chose England's best available players. However, when you look at the options available you can see that England's challenge balances on the smallest of ledges and is dependent on the gods looking favourably on the team. That some of the precariousness is due to the structure of English football is an unacceptable state of affairs.

Capello's insistence that he would pick only players who were on form, were playing regular first-team football and were fully fit went out of the window when he surveyed the wreckage of a season where no proper rest was built in to aid players to prepare for the biggest of tournaments.

Compare this to the three-week Christmas break given to Germany's players. It is said that Germany always do well in World Cups – well, there is a reason for that and it is preparation.

Those who champion the Premier League as the best in the world should also ask – why is it that it cannot produce just two English players in each position, both unarguably of international standard?

Defensively Capello has chosen six centre-backs, three left-backs and one right-back. Without even knowing the team or the players, that bald statistic shows that an injury at right-back leaves a problem.

When you add to this the knowledge that the right-back is Glen Johnson, who is not the most renowned defender in world football, you know things are not ideal to start with.

When you add that cover is likely to be given by Jamie Carragher you really have got issues. Carragher's case is founded on two points – firstly, the fact that he used to play there and second that he is cover for three centre-backs, Terry, Rio Ferdinand and Ledley King, none of whom you can say for certain will last the tournament.

The first observation to make about this state of affairs is that England should not have to go into any tournament without two specialist players in every position. Making do is not good enough when you compete with the rest of the world. Further, Carragher's form has not been good enough this season to justify a role as first-choice replacement for the centre-back position.

Finally, any player who refuses to play for his country should not be given the chance thereafter. Any other stance can be called pragmatism; it can also be called a betrayal of principle and what signal does it send out about the minor accolade of representing your country?

Are we now a nation that in footballing terms has no pride in what representing England means? Is all to be sacrificed on the altar of convenience? This is a widespread view among football fans and yet in this regard the media have given the point of view little or no prominence; it is a much bigger and more noteworthy point than Capello's website.

Defensively England could, with one unfortunate clash of bones, find themselves with at best a makeshift back four and behind them no goalkeeper that can demonstrate ability, form and experience; all of which have been present with previous selections in that position.

Midfield gives no similar concern, although Steven Gerrard's form has to come back for him to retain his place and without Joe Cole there is no spark of inventiveness.

Aaron Lennon should be retained but the advocacy for Shaun Wright-Phillips and Theo Walcott is not firmly based. The last two mentioned have only attracted interest as to whether they will start for their clubs and neither has demonstrated anything other than flashes of potential.

Up front Capello has to pray that Wayne Rooney lasts for the whole of England's challenge because the other players are not among the world's leading strikers.

Darren Bent, Peter Crouch, Jermain Defoe or Emile Heskey: none of these players has regularly gained accolades in the Premier League, let alone at international level, and they have not been tried in combination for any meaningful number of games.

With a fit first XI, England may have a chance of winning the World Cup; with anything less they are doomed to repeat the past years of hurt and the golden generation will have been squandered.

90

If Hugh Robertson is canny, he could save money and boost sport

May 2010

Hugh Robertson, the Conservative sports minister, has made it clear that the Football Association cannot expect a quiet life from the new Government. In the wake of the humiliating resignation of Lord Triesman, Robertson has said that all the football authorities – the FA, Premier League and Football League – should indicate a willingness to reform or face Government intervention. Robertson is especially anxious to see a resolution to the tension that exists between the FA and Premier League and wants reform of the FA's old-fashioned committee culture, still structured around the ninety-two-member FA Council.

It is to be hoped that his determination does not wane under the pressure of everyday trivialities. Now, more than ever, the FA needs an independent voice to counter the dominant ambitions of the professional game.

Robertson will also have to fight hard under the new regime of austerity to prevent sport being the victim of large cuts in spending and it is here that we will see whether he has the right mettle. It is vital that Robertson proves to have the guile and the guts to stand his corner because the full extent of the effect of the recession on sport is becoming apparent.

A Central Council of Physical Recreation survey last year found that, of the sports clubs polled, half were feeling the effects of the recession, with almost the same amount believing that the situation would get worse. Although the feared meltdown has not occurred, conditions have not improved since the survey and a raft of cutbacks and tax increases is going to bite within the next few months.

As a result of the recession, clubs are reducing investment in coaching, kit and facilities, and community initiatives are being postponed or cancelled outright.

Membership renewals have yet to recover properly from the 39 per cent fall in 2009 and new memberships are falling, which means the previous Government's target of getting a million more people into sport by the time of the 2012 Olympic and Paralympic Games is looking increasingly wistful.

With contributions from individual members falling, clubs have looked for corporate assistance but business support is likewise reduced and no sign of a recovery to previous levels is expected soon. Figures are not yet available to judge whether the CCPR warning that as many as six thousand sports clubs were facing the possibility of closure this year are accurate. However, while losing one club is regrettable, the loss of a few thousand would be catastrophic for sport in the UK.

If support is not given to struggling clubs it will mean that the Olympic effect so eagerly awaited as a unique boost for UK sport will be lost. Already the Government is looking to reduce spending on the 2012 Games and the legacy, which was one of the principal reasons for London winning the bid, will be impossible to achieve if insufficient sports clubs exist for converts to play sport. While no area of spending can be sacrosanct, sport has a powerful case to fight Treasury cuts because of the proximity and nature of this opportunity. Grass-roots sport has to be given life support now to tide it through this recession, because once clubs fail they cannot be resurrected easily, like some building project.

Nick Clegg, the Deputy Prime Minister, announced on Tuesday that there will be a bonfire of unwarranted laws and regulations.

Robertson should seize on this initiative to try to effect some simple measures that would assist sport without costing much. In fact, in some cases they would actually save some money. For example, to prevent further loss of playing fields he should press for sports fields to be a specific land category (as is the case with agricultural land) that has clear planning restrictions on use and development. This would enable users to better prevent local councils, in cahoots with developers, from taking yet more playing fields from us. A further dissuading measure would be to apply full rates to sports clubs that are acquired by developers and then left fallow.

The mandatory granting of shared use of school facilities, including private schools, with local sports clubs would reduce costs and the maintenance of a school's charitable status should be linked to such access.

Equally worrying, if not more so, the CCPR report highlighted a drop in the numbers of volunteers at clubs, with more than a fifth of clubs saying that present circumstances have had a negative or very negative impact on attracting and retaining volunteers. This is predictable: when people have less money to spend, volunteering always costs something, even if it is just travel, but one thing which is going to make the situation an awful lot worse are the new requirements of the Independent Safeguarding Authority (ISA).

If you want to do your bit and you are involved in what is called a regulated or controlled activity – basically any activity of a specified nature that involves contact with children or vulnerable adults – you are required to register with the ISA and subject yourself to their 'vetting and barring' scheme.

Applying for registration will require detailed personal information being requested and then retained on a database, to which will be added any comments from other parties, such as the police, local authorities, employers and so on. You will also have registered against you any 'soft' intelligence anybody wishes to place on your record – unsubstantiated claims, rumours and the like.

While well intentioned, this initiative is deeply flawed. It will do nothing for victims of predators and will not catch anyone who has not already been caught. A simple national database of offenders would have been sufficient for preventing the convicted from working with the vulnerable. Moreover, it would save tens of millions of pounds annually.

As it is, this may prove even more of a hurdle for sport than a poor economy. With this coalition Government's alleged zeal for setting the citizen free from bureaucracy, Robertson must concentrate on the small but significant measures that will make a vast difference to UK sport. On a macro level, he must also prevent encroachment from other departments seeking to offload responsibilities for social behaviour projects on to sport.

Finally, and as an absolute priority, he must keep the Treasury's hands off National Lottery funding. It is not tax revenue – and not Government property.

Index

Brian Moore won sixty-four caps for the England rugby team between 1987 and 1995. He played in three Rugby World Cups and won the Grand Slam in 1991, 1992 and 1995. He went on two British Lions tours. Originally a qualified solicitor, he writes for the *Sun* and the *Telegraph* newspapers and is a co-commentator for international rugby matches alongside Eddie Butler on BBC TV.